HOPE
FOR THE
PERFECTIONIST
Dr. David Stoop

THE MINIRTH-MEIER CLINIC OFFICES

National Headquarters
MINIRTH-MEIER CLINIC, P.A.
2100 N. Collins Blvd.
Richardson, Texas 75080
(214) 669-1733
1-800-229-3000
OUTPATIENT SERVICES
DAY TREATMENT CENTER
HOSPITAL PROGRAMS
NATIONAL MEDIA
  MINISTRIES

MINIRTH-MEIER CLINIC,
P.C.
The Grove, Suite 1510
2100 Manchester Road
Wheaton, Illinois 60187
(708) 653-1717
1-800-848-8872
1-800-545-1819
OUTPATIENT SERVICES
DAY TREATMENT CENTER
HOSPITAL PROGRAMS
NATIONAL
  COMMUNICATIONS
  DIVISION

MINIRTH-MEIER TUNNELL
& WILSON CLINIC
Centre Creek Office Plaza,
  Suite 200
1812 Centre Creek Drive
Austin, Texas 78754
(512) 339-7511
1-800-444-5751
OUTPATIENT SERVICES
DAY TREATMENT CENTER
HOSPITAL PROGRAMS

MINIRTH-MEIER-RICE
CLINIC, P.A.
Koger Center in the Shannon
  Building
10801 Executive Center Drive,
  Suite 305
Little Rock, Arkansas 72211
(501) 225-0576
1-800-488-4769
OUTPATIENT SERVICES
HOSPITAL PROGRAMS

MINIRTH-MEIER CLINIC
WEST
260 Newport Center Drive,
  Suite 430
Newport Beach, California 92660
(714) 760-3112
1-800-877-4673
OUTPATIENT SERVICES
DAY TREATMENT CENTER
HOSPITAL PROGRAMS

MINIRTH-MEIER BYRD
CLINIC, P.A.
4300 Fair Lakes Court, Suite 200
Fairfax, Virginia 22033-4231
(703) 968-3556
1-800-486-HOPE (4673)
OUTPATIENT SERVICES
DAY TREATMENT CENTER
HOSPITAL PROGRAMS

For general information about other Minirth-Meier Clinic branch offices, counseling services, educational resources and hospital programs, call toll-free **1-800-545-1819.**

National Headquarters: (214) 669-1733   1-800-229-3000

HOPE FOR THE PERFEC- TIONIST

Dr. David Stoop

❖ *A Janet Thoma Book* ❖

THOMAS NELSON PUBLISHERS
Nashville

❖ A Janet Thoma Book ❖

Published in Nashville, Tennessee, by Oliver-Nelson Books, a division of Thomas Nelson, Inc., Publishers, and distributed in Canada by Lawson Falle, Ltd., Cambridge, Ontario.

Unless otherwise noted, the Bible version used in this publication is THE NEW KING JAMES VERSION. Copyright © 1979, 1980, 1982, Thomas Nelson, Inc., Publishers.

Verses marked TLB are taken from *The Living Bible*, copyright 1971 by Tyndale House Publishers, Wheaton, IL. Used by permission.

Fig. 4. TUMBLEWEEDS by Tom K. Ryan © Field Enterprises, Inc. 1981. Permission of News America Syndicate.

Fig. 7. Graph by William Criddle, from RATIONAL LIVING Magazine, vol. 10, 1975. Used by permission.

Fig. 8. Pleasure-Perfection Balance Sheet. REPRINTED WITH PERMISSION FROM PSYCHOLOGY TODAY MAGAZINE Copyright © 1980 American Psychological Association.

The persons described in this volume represent a composite of Dr. David Stoop's practice, and no one individual is portrayed.

Printed in the United States.

6 7 — 96 95 94 93

Library of Congress Cataloging-in-Publication Data

Stoop, David A.
    Hope for the perfectionist / David Stoop.
      p.   cm.
    Rev. ed. of: Living with a perfectionist. c1987.
    Includes bibliographical references.
    ISBN 0-8407-9600-5
    1. Perfectionism (Personality trait). 2. Interpersonal relations.
  I. Stoop, David A. Living with a perfectionist. II. Title.
BF698.35.P47S76 1991
155.2'32—dc20
                                         91–23785
                                           CIP

*To Jan
—my favorite perfectionist—
and to all the other perfectionists
who have given me insight
into their world.*

David Stoop, Ph.D., is a clinical psychologist in private practice in Newport Beach, California, and is the clinical director of the Minirth-Meier-Stoop Clinic and a program director for the Minirth-Meier Clinic West, a psychiatric treatment program. His other books include *When Someone You Love is Someone You Hate; Forgiving Our Parents, Forgiving Ourselves;* and *Self-Talk*. He and his wife, Jan, have three sons and two granddaughters. They live in Newport Beach.

CONTENTS

ACKNOWLEDGMENTS

*M*any perfectionists have helped me understand the issues they struggle with. I want to express my deep appreciation for the time they gave and the insights I received from them. Some, like Victor Oliver, and my friend Stephen Arterburn, took the time to prod me, interact with me, and encourage me along the way. along the way.

And then there are those who filled out our lengthy questionnaire—I want to say thank you to them all: Connie, Carol, Susan, Carl, Frank, Jim, Robert, Diane, Barry, Linda, Robert, Karen, Marcia, Ruth, Sally, Bill, Donna, Stephen, Gloria, Vern, Pam, Thomas, Christine, Denise, Susan, Janet, Dianne, Pat, and Liane.

I especially appreciate the help that Martha Greene provided as she researched the journals and worked with me on the organization of the book. My family tolerated my own perfectionistic tendency to procrastinate. Not only was Jan understanding, but she walked with me through each page as well.

To each, a big thank you!

PREFACE

Anything that's really worth doing is worth doing badly.
—*G. K. Chesterton*

Most of us live with a perfectionist. That perfectionist may be a spouse, a parent, a sibling, or even one of our children. Or we may live with a perfectionist only during the part of the day called "work," where the perfectionist is a boss or a coworker. But many of us live with one all the time, for often the perfectionist we may live with is ourself.

Perfectionists are those who idealize almost everything around them. They set up standards and images for themselves and others that are impossible to meet. They find that much of their time and energy is spent trying to meet these expectations and trying to control their environment. And the people around the perfectionists are expected to work just as hard at meeting those standards.

Perfectionism hangs like a cloud over a large percentage of us. Perfectionists live under pressure, and they have difficulty breaking those behavior patterns. To perfectionists, anything around that needs to be done is worth doing perfectly. To them, Chesterton's quote would be considered, at worst, totally absurd, and at best, a silly joke. But to the English literature professor who gave me that quote, Chesterton's insight was a breath of fresh air in the frustrating world of his perfectionism.

On first thought, perfectionism appeared to me as a positive virtue. But the more I listened to people in my counseling practice, the more I heard the pain and frustration related to perfectionism. I started asking questions and without exception found that perfectionism is a subtle trap that quickly becomes a prison. Perfectionism makes no one happier.

As I talked with Jan, the perfectionist I live with, I started to develop a little pride in the fact that I wasn't a perfectionist. For years I had been telling Jan to just relax, to not worry. Now I could add to my "helpful" suggestions the idea that if she kept on trying to do everything perfectly, she'd only end up unhappier. Obviously, that wasn't too helpful. You can't simply tell a perfectionist to ease up on something. Convincing a perfectionist to change is not that simple. So be forewarned: *You cannot use any information in this book as ammunition in your private battle against perfectionism.* If you do, it is absolutely guaranteed to make things worse—for you *and* your target.

So why should you read this book if you are not a perfectionist? Let me suggest three reasons. First, if you read the book, the perfectionist you live with might be interested in what you are reading. Second, you will find in this book information that will help you to understand better the private world of the perfectionist. Perfectionism is a complex behavior pattern that will not yield to simple directives. Its roots go deep, and changes can be worked out only in an atmosphere of understanding and acceptance. Use this information for the purpose of understanding the perfectionist, not for the purpose of *changing* the perfectionist.

Third, you may find out that you, a nonperfectionist, really have some areas of perfectionism in your own life. My pride at not being a perfectionist faded the longer Jan and I talked together. She helped me to see that I had areas of perfectionism that I had never acknowledged. Because those areas were blind spots for me, they often created tension or problems in my life that limited what I was trying to accomplish. I needed to look honestly at those areas to see how they were affecting my life. You may find it valuable to do the same thing.

Moroccans make rugs with deliberate imperfections. Designs are purposely woven with "mistakes" in the pattern. Rug makers believe it is either ludicrous or blasphemous to attempt perfection when only God is perfect, and flaws are seen as reminders that humans are only human. *Hope For the Perfectionist* is similarily imperfect (although for quite a while I was convinced it had to be perfect). I hope it will give you permission to accept the flaws and foibles in your life that only show you are human after all.

DAVID STOOP
NEWPORT BEACH, CALIFORNIA

Who Are the Perfectionists?

People with perfectionistic values are true children of our individualistic society.
—Brian L.

*I*t wasn't that I was looking for perfectionism to be a problem, it just seemed to keep cropping up as an issue with almost everyone who came to me for counseling. Cindy is a good example.

The first time she came into the office, she nervously sat on the edge of the couch for the whole session. I watched her as I listened to what she was saying, and at one point I commented, "It looks to me like you are almost ready to jump up and run out the door."

She was quick to admit that that was exactly what she was feeling, and added, "In fact, I wish I could jump up and just run anywhere. My life is totally out of control. I thought I had it all planned so carefully, but no one, including me, is doing what they're supposed to be doing."

I didn't need to ask her to explain, for she quickly went on to tell me about how each of her kids failed to turn out the way she hoped they would and how her husband had comfortably settled into what she termed a rut. All the dreams that she and her husband had talked about early in their marriage were no longer of interest to him. She said her husband couldn't possibly understand the desperation she felt inside. "I have tried to talk to him," she said, "but it is like talking to a brick wall. No one can understand what it's like to be the only one who cares that things are right! Everything is up to me, and I'm tired of trying to do it all, but I don't know how to stop."

The next time Cindy came to see me, I chuckled to myself as I watched her walk in, straighten the cushions on my couch, sit down, and then lean over to pick a piece of lint off the floor that was obviously bothering her. I commented on what she did, and she nervously laughed, saying, "I guess my perfectionism is showing."

"What's it like to be a perfectionist?" I asked.

She was quiet for a while, and then blurted out, "It's painful! At least, most of the time. Sometimes I think it helps me do a better job, but most of the time my perfectionism immobilizes me. I get paralyzed by the fear of failing. So I end up missing out on a lot of new experiences, especially those I can't control."

The more we talked about her perfectionism, the more she talked about the negative aspects of it. At one point she said, "It feels like I am in a cage and I can't get out. I can think about it—about relaxing with things and not worrying about being perfect—but something inside of me just won't allow me to. It seems that if I were to lower my standards, the whole world would fall apart. I don't want to have to worry about the cans all facing the same way in the cupboard, but it really bugs me when someone moves them around. I know that sounds silly, but I can't help it."

I could feel the helplessness she was experiencing as she went on to describe how her perfectionism led to vague, dissatisfied feelings she had toward herself. "My perfectionism keeps me from focusing on my strengths. It doesn't allow me to grow—to be human, to have weaknesses, to have needs," she said. Like other perfectionists, Cindy expected too much of others, but mostly she expected too much of herself. She idealized herself, the world, and all the people in it. She set standards that couldn't be met and then experienced negative feelings for not meeting those standards. Her perfectionism damaged her self-esteem, stunted her emotional growth, closed her off from new personal experiences, and isolated her from other people.

Most relationship problems I encounter in my counseling stem from some form of perfectionism. One woman told me she was either "down" on her husband for not doing things according to her standards or else "biting her tongue" to keep the peace by not openly criticizing him.

A man said, "I am very intolerant of other people's weaknesses. I have to be constantly on guard not to be a tyrant or, perhaps I should say, a constant nag about my family's imperfections. It's very hard for me to hide my disapproval when they 'drop the ball.'" It's not an easy task to live with someone who has these kinds of expectations or with someone who is always holding back in the relationship. It's just not easy to live with a perfectionist.

So who are the perfectionists? Is perfectionism related to personality? That's a question my wife, Jan, and I are often asked at a seminar we present on personality types. Based on a test we give, some people at the seminar are identified as open-ended, spontaneous, and flexible. Others are seen as decisive, structured, and in need of having things finished. At first glance, it would appear that those who are more structured would be the perfectionists and those who are open-ended would not be perfectionistic. As we discussed the subject in the seminar, it became increasingly clearer that personality factors have some effect on who the perfectionists are but that perfectionists are found in every personality style.

Based on this idea, we took a survey to poll people on their attitudes toward perfectionism. Of the 222 people who responded, 84 percent said they were perfectionistic in some way. Only 16 percent claimed to be nonperfectionistic. And personality was not a factor in the results. We found it interesting that several people did not know whether they were perfectionistic or not, but when we asked if their spouses would consider them to be perfectionists, they said yes.

When we check several dictionaries for definitions of the words *perfect, perfectionism,* and *perfectionist,* some words that recur are *flawless, faultless, extreme, obsessive;* that is, perfectionistic behavior seems to include extreme efforts to achieve flawless, faultless performance.

Webster's brings in such ideas as "letter-perfect," "supreme excellence," "ideal standard," and "being saintly." *American Heritage* uses phrases like "undiminished excellence" and "extremely high standards." *Oxford American Dictionary* associates perfectionism with being "satisfied with nothing less than what . . . is perfect."

All of these definitions have in common a sense of absoluteness about the goal, as if one should and must make an extreme, obsessive effort to achieve a flawless, faultless performance or objective.

In our survey, we asked perfectionists how they would define these words. They said:

- "Doing something so well, nothing could make it better."

- "Doing nothing wrong; making no errors."

- "The need to have everything and everyone in just the right order."

- "The unreasonable desire to be perfect in every way."

- "Perfection is a goal which is impossible and leads to frustration."

- "Pushing yourself to reach an impossible goal."

- "Having internal and external levels of expectations, both for myself and others, that are so high as to be unreasonable."

Such goals make one wonder why people would even admit to being perfectionists. One nonperfectionist in the survey wanted to make it very clear that she was *not* a perfectionist. She wrote:

I am not a perfectionist. I don't want to be perfect. I'm tired of people who are always talking about feeling guilty because they are not perfect; it makes me feel guilty that I don't feel guilty about not wanting to be perfect. (But not guilty enough to do anything about it.)

She probably lives with a perfectionist!

These are contemporary attitudes and definitions, but a look back through history tells us the problem has been around for a long time. A French senator is quoted as saying to Napoleon, "Sire, the desire for perfection is one of the worst maladies that can affect the human mind!" The nineteenth-century French poet and writer Alfred de Musset said, "Perfection does not exist; to understand it is the triumph of human intelligence; to expect to possess it is the most dangerous kind of madness." Friedrich Holderlin, the eighteenth-century German poet, wrote that "what has made the state into hell is that man wanted to make it his heaven." He was echoing the words of Aristotle, who wrote, "The essence of political tragedy is to make the perfect the enemy of the good."

Not everyone has seen perfectionism in a negative light. Lord Chesterfield said we are to "aim at perfection in everything, though in most things it is unattainable." Then he added as motivation, "However, they who aim at it, and persevere will come much nearer to it than those whose laziness and despondency make them give it up as unattainable." Perhaps perfectionism is seen as a motivational factor against laziness. These are just a few of the quotes about perfectionism I found early in my research in this area.

As I delved further, I became interested in how much and how often perfectionism was related to other problems. I became more aware of the perfectionistic traits in people who were coming to me for counseling; of how often they were struggling with this issue. If someone didn't say something about perfectionism right away, I would ask if that was a part of the struggle. Invariably, the response was positive. I found that woven into the fabric of almost every problem that people brought to me was a pattern of perfectionism.

One of the clearest threads in that pattern was the notion of the "shoulds"—or what psychologist Karen Horney called *the tyranny of the "shoulds."*[1] These inner dictates about how people "should" be can become controlling, and they are at the heart of perfectionism.

One woman, who was the mother of seven children, found that a big part of the hassles she experienced had to do with the multitude of "shoulds" she had about herself and her family. She believed that to be a good mother, she had to be a perfect mother. And to achieve this, she had a long list of what she should or should not do, what each child should or should not do, and what her husband should or should not do.

She told herself things like, "I should volunteer to be a room mother for Gary's class this year." *(I don't have enough time now, but I need to show that I care.)* "Marilyn should wear skirts instead of jeans to school." *(She says everyone wears jeans and that the school doesn't care, but when I was in school I always dressed properly. So should she.)* "Jerry should remember our anniversary without my having to tell him each year." *(He would if he really loved me.)*

We spent much time together as she learned how to release these expectations. About every six months after that, she would make an appointment, come in, sit down, and say, "Tell me about the 'shoulds' again."

I was often asked to speak on the subject of the "shoulds" and the thought patterns related to them. I found that as people understood the effect of the words they said to others and to themselves, they experienced a greater freedom in their lives. And as they understood the incredible negative effect of the "shoulds," they began to break some of the perfectionistic behavior patterns in their lives. A lot of what I taught was with that perfectionistic mother of seven children in mind.

But not everybody I talked with was able to break

the pattern of "shoulds" in the thought patterns. Not every aspect of perfectionism can be explained by an individual's thoughts. Take Ron, for example. He doesn't think about trying to do things perfectly, he just strives for it "almost naturally." His appearance leaves no room for criticism. He dresses impeccably. His pants never seem to have a wrinkle in them. His shoes are *always* freshly polished. His shirt sleeves show precisely a half inch below his jacket sleeves. The colors are all perfectly coordinated. In fact, everything about him is neat and clean—his desk, his home, even his car, which is probably cleaner now than when he bought it.

Out in his garage, Ron has a workshop. He used to work with wood, but he kept taking longer and longer to finish his projects. And his dissatisfaction with the mess the sawdust made along the way, along with the imperfect end result, led him to taking even longer to make anything; eventually, he hesitated to begin anything. Everyone else admired his work, but all he could see were the minute flaws that were almost invisible. All he does now in his garage is clean the bench and the tools.

If we could listen to Ron's thoughts, we would hear his continual criticism of himself and his constant search for the flaws in anything he attempts to do. Inside, there is no pride or joy in what he accomplishes, only the haunting fear that someone will find something wrong with what he has done. Even though we can find perfectionistic thought patterns in Ron, his behavior seems to be motivated more by the fear that someone will find a fatal flaw in him.

Ben isn't much different from Ron. His garage is immaculate, too. In fact, he has framed pictures hanging on its walls as if it is another room inside the house. He has sheets of plastic taped to the garage floor so he can quickly wipe clean any fluids that drip from his car. His wife, Mary, recently bought him some jogging shoes with Velcro fasteners because she was so frustrated with his need to have the shoelaces all neatly arranged at just the right angles to the shoes in the closet. Every night when he takes his glasses off and empties his pockets, he neatly arranges each item in a geometric pattern on top of his dresser. Living with him isn't easy. Mary just loves to brush against one of the items and spoil the perfectly geometric arrangement.

One time when Mary was out of town, Ben thought he would help her get organized. He very carefully cleaned the cupboards in the kitchen and put in plain white shelf paper. As he replaced each item in the cupboard, he drew the shape on the shelf paper and then wrote in the name of the item. He thought Mary would be delighted with such an easy plan to keep the cupboards organized perfectly. She wasn't thrilled, to say the least!

Sarah might have welcomed the kind of help Ben had offered his wife. Sarah is a "superwoman." She goes nonstop all day. She's into the parents organization at the kids' school, sings in the church choir, spends some time as a volunteer at the hospital, is room mother for her oldest child, substitute teaches in Sunday school, sews all of her own clothes as well as the kids', and keeps a spotless home. The first thing she does every morning and the last thing she does when she finally stops late at night is clean the kitchen sink. "I just like things clean," she protested when a friend threatened to come by to look at her new house before she moved in. Her friend said, "It's probably the last time a speck of dirt will be allowed inside." Even though Sarah says she would like to loosen up a bit, she doesn't know how.

Her medical doctor suggested she come for counseling because he felt that many of her physical problems were related to the stress she puts on herself. At first she resisted the idea, but she finally agreed to follow his advice. She has found it difficult to look at the cycle she's caught in that keeps pushing her to do better than her best at everything.

When she sews something, every stitch and every seam must be perfect. If it is not, she will usually tear it out and do it over. In her closet, every hanger matches and is turned the same way. In her cupboards, the dog food cans and all the others are right side up with the labels faced to the front. When she takes charge of doing something, either at the church or at the school, it's hard to find people willing to work with her. They are afraid they won't measure up to her standards. But those who volunteered in the past found that there was little fear of messing up—Sarah did everything.

Andrea is similar to Sarah in some ways, but different in others. She's not a superwoman because there are lots of things she won't do for fear of failure. She is convinced that if she does anything poorly, it will be proof that she is totally inadequate or bad as a person. She dresses perfectly, making certain that everything matches perfectly. Her purse can't just be close in color to her shoes, it must be exactly the same, even though the salesclerk points out that no one will ever see them against each other. For Andrea, close isn't good enough.

She spends a lot of time procrastinating. If she thinks the kitchen needs cleaning, she is convinced it needs a complete cleaning. Everything she experiences is in terms of all or nothing. If she is going to clean anything, it must be thoroughly and completely cleaned and reorganized. When she finally gets to the task of cleaning the kitchen her way, she empties the cupboards so she can completely reorganize them. Of course, she is usually interrupted in the process, and she has to jam everything back into the cupboards or the drawers.

She does the same with her closet. She can't decide whether to organize it by color, by item, by use, or by season. Every time she attempts to clean it, she tries a different way to organize it.

If she finally gets either the kitchen or her closet cleaned, the most frustrating part for her is what to do with the things left over. Where can she put all the extra odds and ends that had been crammed into the drawers in the kitchen? What does she do with the piles of clothes from the closet now sitting on the bedroom floor? Fortunately, the pressures of life don't allow her to do such thorough and complete cleaning very often. And then, too, she can talk about and think about these things for a long period of time because she is often too paralyzed by her need to do it all so perfectly that she ends up not doing anything at all.

Part of Andrea's problem is that she sets such unrealistic goals for herself that either she is discouraged before she starts, or she puts off starting because of the amount of time required to accomplish her goal perfectly. Her friends suggest that she set more realistic goals for herself. She usually answers with something like, "Yes, that would probably be better, but I just can't." In fact, *can't* is one of the most common words in her thought patterns.

Each of these people—Ron, Ben, Sarah, and Andrea—would admit to being a perfectionist. No one would doubt that. I personally don't know Ron, Ben, Sarah, or Andrea, for they are really composites of a number of perfectionists I have talked with. Maybe you know someone like them. Maybe you share some perfectionistic patterns with them. Think about these four people, and then think about yourself. How much of a perfectionist would you say you are? After you have thought about this for a moment, rate yourself on the self-rating scale below:

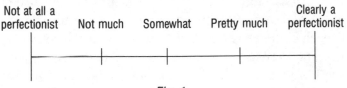

Fig. 1.

After you have rated yourself, talk with people who know you well, and ask them if they agree with your rating. Where would they place you on the scale?

We found in our survey that people had some difficulty rating themselves about their perfectionism. Some thought that since they were perfectionistic only in certain areas of life, they were not perfectionists. It was as if they were saying, "If I'm not a complete perfectionist, I don't have any problem with perfectionism." Based on what we found in that first survey, we developed a long list of questions that we gave to a group of people who scored high as perfectionists. A number of the quotes in this book are taken from their responses. We were amazed at how interested perfectionists were in helping us with our research. People called us to ask if they could help. One person stopped Jan at the store to ask if he could answer the questions. Each of them has eagerly been waiting to see what we found out in our research. (Part of me is afraid that their perfectionism will make them look for every flaw in the book—but so be it.)

In the studies done by Dr. David Burns, he reports that about half the population or more would be "clearly a perfectionist."[2] In our survey, we found that over 80 percent were "somewhat a perfectionist" and were likely to struggle with perfectionism in certain broad areas of their lives, in ways similar to Andrea's approach to cleaning her closet and kitchen. The other 20 percent were found at the extremes. Those scoring on the low end were likely to have specific "pockets" of perfectionism, and those scoring on the high end were likely to experience pervasive perfectionism in their lives.

Figure 2 shows some of the statements we used in our survey. Before reading on, check whether you agree or disagree with the statements. The number of statements you agree with—and the way they affect

AGREE   DISAGREE

		1. I often put things off because I don't have time to do them perfectly.
		2. I expect the best of myself at all times.
		3. I generally think I could have done it better.
		4. I get upset when things don't go as planned.
		5. Other people can't understand my desire to do things right.
		6. I am often disappointed in the quality of other people's work.
		7. I feel my standards should be the highest possible, allowing for a clarity of direction and a standard of performance.
		8. If anything I do is considered average, I'm unhappy.
		9. I think less of myself if I repeat a mistake.

Fig. 2.

your life—are an indicator of your perfectionistic tendencies.

Most people deny their perfectionism and defend it as the "norm," and they are so accustomed to their behavior in this area that they no longer consider it to be perfectionistic.

What do we mean when we refer to "pockets" of perfectionism? These are specific areas that individuals are perfectionists about, even though they are not perfectionists about any other areas of their lives. Perfectionists identified these "pocket" areas for us, and nothing was exempt. Work was mentioned most often. Home and relationships followed closely behind in frequency. Other areas identified were hobbies; problem solving; thinking; what I say to others; sex life; entertaining; shopping; organization; school work; appearance, including weight and physical conditioning; schedule; car; spiritual life; and the little things. One person summed it up by saying, "I expect to be perfect in my home life, work life, and social life." Not much else is left! Another area mentioned was motives—they wanted to be certain that all of their motives were absolutely pure.

One perfectionist said she wanted to be perfect in the area of her weaknesses. If it is an impossible task to be perfect in the area of strengths, it must feel awfully hopeless to her to believe that she must be perfect in her weaknesses. Another respondent said that he was a perfectionist at making certain other people do things perfectly.

There appears to be something about perfectionism that makes people feel uneasy when they face the subject. Though sometimes glorified, perfectionism is not a positive virtue. At best, most people consider it a mixed blessing that sometimes leads to procrastinating and always seems to produce guilt. At worst, it lures many individuals into the seductive and fatal path of substance abuse and physical illnesses, including anorexia nervosa. Regardless of the attitude toward it, perfectionism presents a dilemma. David Burns describes it like this:

> **Think of it this way—there are two doors to enlightenment. One is marked "Perfection," and the other is marked "Average." The "Perfection" door is ornate, fancy, and destructive. It tempts you. You want very much to go through it. The "Average" door seems drab and plain. Ugh! Who wants it?**
>
> **So you try to go through the "Perfection" door and always discover a brick wall on the other side. As you insist on trying to break through, you only end up with a sore nose and a headache. On the other side of the "Average" door, in contrast, there's a magic garden. But it may never have occurred to you to open this door and take a look!**[3]

Every perfectionist I have talked with will attest to the frustration described by Burns. In fact, it can often be one of the most disturbing emotional problems experienced because the frustration is intensified by an apparent inability to break out of the vicious cycle.

The door of "Perfection" leads into anxiety, self-deprecation, discouragement, and a compulsive emphasis on the externals of life. Those who seek to enter that door end up reaching for impossible dreams and goals. In the end, they find only a conditional experience of love and life. I can't count the number of perfectionists who have told me that the possibility that anything less than the perfect can be good is just "too good to be true." No amount of persuasion can get them to change their minds.

Even though perfectionists know that their behaviors are self-defeating and take away the joy of living, they hang on. They press on, trying harder, not realizing that we human beings "cannot relax if we are constantly demanding too much of ourselves, if our emotions are out of control, if we are unhappy because our reach exceeds our grasp."[4]

But then, where do high standards fit into this picture? Most perfectionists believe that trying harder is really striving for excellence. The line between excellence and perfectionism is difficult to discern. The perfectionist often starts out in a search for excellence and then moves into the area of perfectionism, reaching for an illusion—an ideal that is yet to be achieved in reality. To better understand how someone crosses over this line, we need to look first at the inner world of the perfectionist.

The World of the Perfectionist

As a perfectionist, I have never found any
contentment in my life—no place to rest.

*I*n the novel *Moby Dick,* Herman Melville painted a
vivid picture of Captain Ahab and his quest to destroy
Moby Dick, the great white whale. Ahab was *totally*
possessed by his desire, and he directed all his energies to that one end. Ahab could find no rest, no
contentment—much like the perfectionist quoted
above—until Moby Dick was dead. Nothing could deter
him from the mad course he had chosen. Although
many people tried to persuade him to give up his in-
sane pursuit, he listened to no one; his resolve re-
mained to the end just as it was in the beginning. His
was a relentless pursuit of one thing to the exclusion of
everything else. And it resulted, ultimately, in his
death.

Captain Ahab suffered from an extreme form of one
of the main characteristics of a perfectionist—he
thought in terms of polarities. Life was all-or-nothing

to him. If he could not succeed in his one goal, life was meaningless to him, and he believed himself to be a failure. That's why he persisted to the bitter end. His behavior repeated itself with no alteration or deviation in spite of the warnings and in spite of his knowledge of the impossibility of the task. The captain knew the danger—he bore the scars from previous battles with the great whale and had lost a leg in one encounter. Even another sea captain who had lost his arm to the white whale could do nothing to sway Ahab's determination.

When at last the whale was sighted, Ahab battled it for two days, losing both boats and men. He persisted on to that fatal third day, when all but Ishmael, the narrator, were killed.

DICHOTOMOUS THINKING

Like other perfectionists, Ahab suffered from either-or thinking. This style of thinking breaks everything into dichotomies, where everything is either in one class or in its opposite. Behavior is based on the idea that "either I am my ideal or I am its opposite (or something else negative such as 'mediocre'). . . . Either I am *perfectly* (successful, outstanding, intelligent, competent) or I am the opposite of my ideal."[1]

Other examples of either-or thinking are "either I'm a straight-A student or I'm too dumb to learn" or "either I'm a good mother or I'm a bad mother" or "either

I'm popular or I'm a nerd" or "either I'm a great artist or I'm wasting my time even trying." In this process, perfectionists develop an absolutistic attitude about themselves, believing that it is unacceptable to have *any* degree of some "negative" quality, such as jealousy, anger, or selfishness, or any kind of "negative" behaviors: "If I show anger, then I am an awful person. If I act in a selfish way in one situation, I am a terrible, bad, selfish person."

This either-or kind of thinking is evident in the way perfectionists describe their feelings:

- "I love my perfectionism, and I hate it. It is what drives me and at the same time causes endless amounts of frustration."

- "I view my perfectionism as both good and bad. Good because it helps me do things well, but bad in that I sometimes don't do anything because I don't want to do less than perfect."

There is an either-or theme running through these quotes and through the thoughts of perfectionists. Either something is perfect, or it is worthless. Either it is all-black, or it is all-white. There is no in-between. This split between the good and the bad is what keeps perfectionists striving, for the alternative is to be totally worthless. These statements by perfectionists support this view:

- "I hate it because I don't like being imperfect! I don't attempt many things at all because of my fear of failure."

- "It hinders me in trying new things or sticking with old things. . . . I hate it because I waste so much energy trying to do better. The things I do achieve aren't good enough, or I don't have any energy left, after worrying, to try to achieve anything."

- "I rationalize my failures—I don't get in touch with my true feelings."

Dichotomous thinking leads to several distorted patterns. First, there is the tendency to look too much to the future and develop what is called the *hurdle effect.*[2] This is seen in the preceding quotes, when the speaker refuses to try anything because of the possibility of failure. By looking at the future, perfectionists see only the hurdles ahead that would limit performance. Their either-or thinking blinds them to their past accomplishments—they choose to look only at the barriers in the future. They end up paralyzed by what they perceive to be insurmountable roadblocks.

Second, perfectionists practice what is called *Maximizing and Minimizing.*[3] This M & M pattern will maximize failure and minimize success. When a goal has been met in the past, it is minimized or seen as relatively unimportant. When asked if he was ever satisfied with something he had done, one perfectionist an-swered, "Oh, yes, but those 'somethings' I was satisfied with were *only* small 'perfect' steps to the larger, and more important, perfect goal." Another person said, "Sometimes I feel satisfied, but never completely. I can think of maybe one time when I was completely satisfied." Both people would quickly minimize any success they had, pointing out the magnitude of the problems they still face.

In relationships, this M & M pattern can be seen where approval is being sought from another person, but when the approving statement is made, it is quickly minimized and neutralized. "You look lovely" is quickly countered with "My hair is awful, it didn't come out right."

In business, it can be seen in the secretary who stays late every time she is asked because she is afraid that if she doesn't stay late *this time*, she will be fired. Or in the sales manager who has had the best sales month ever, but is depressed because his division still isn't the top one in the company.

A third way that perfectionists participate in dichotomous thinking is the tendency to give a *negative attribution*[4] to other people's motives or behaviors. This means that perfectionists focus on someone's body language or tone of voice or some other subtle behavior as evidence of a negative attitude toward them. No matter what, they are able to find some reason to think other people feel negative about them. In reality, they are attributing their own negative feelings about themselves to other persons.

Often a rigid, legalistic approach to life follows dichotomous thinking patterns. Perfectionists make lists, either on paper or in the mind, as an attempt to control both their behavior and their environment. In some people, this attempt to control leads to ritualistic behavior and even avoidant or phobic behaviors. Their all-or-nothing, either-or thinking drives them to one extreme in behavior and often to the other extreme in their attitudes about themselves and others.

Let one ripple stir the waters of tranquillity in relationships, and the perfectionist either gets to work to smooth things out or assumes that the person causing the ripple is terrible, cruel, and totally unworthy of any more contact. Either it is all peace and harmony, or it is awful! One perfectionist told me how she had to keep changing friends. Whenever she was disappointed by a friend, she completely cut off any more contact with that person.

UNREALISTIC GOALS

Closely associated with dichotomous thinking is the second characteristic of perfectionists, which is the tendency to set unrealistic goals for themselves and for others. Benjamin Franklin provides an example of this. His "most ambitious behavior-modification project was aimed at changing his own behavior. 'I wished to live,' he wrote, 'without committing any fault at any time.' " Even the most ardent perfectionist would have to agree that Franklin had set an unrealistic goal for himself. But Franklin persisted, stating that "as I knew, or thought I knew, what was right and wrong, I did not see why I might not *always* do the one and avoid the other."[5] He decided to break his bad habits and build or strengthen his good ones. He compiled a list of thirteen virtues, complete with descriptions of the conduct they designated.

Franklin's plan was to work a thirteen-week cycle, spending a week on each virtue. He apparently thought that after several cycles, he would be very nearly perfect. Later on, Franklin was the first to admit that he was unable to fulfill his plan.

Like a man who grows weary of polishing a rusty ax to perfection, he found himself drawn to consider the merits of a "speckled ax." "A perfect character," he wrote, "might be attended with the inconvenience of being envied and hated; . . . a benevolent man should allow a few faults in himself, to keep his friends in countenance."[6]

Franklin had the wisdom to revise his unrealistic goals—a wisdom few perfectionists seem to possess. Most set unrealistic goals for themselves and end up blaming themselves for their failures and feeling totally frustrated. In their minds they hear old statements like, "Your sister got better grades than that." "Why don't you make something out of your life?" "Winning is everything, so give it everything you have!" "Nobody in our family has ever settled for less." Perfectionists most likely do not realize how these messages have been internalized to make their lives so unmanageable.

In an article entitled "The Misery of Perfectionism,"[7] Paul Rom states that all too often perfectionists end up nervous, self-conscious, and self-critical, and they also discourage others and alienate others from themselves. They become isolated human beings, longing to relate in a friendly manner but unable to develop long-lasting friendships. Our respondents agreed, stating:

- "I wish I wasn't a perfectionist. Sometimes I feel controlled by it. I wish I was more relaxed about things and other people."

- "I do everything better than anyone else. I am respected, *but* I have no close friends—no one I can trust."

- "I believe that my perfectionism has cut down on the number of close friends I have as an adult."

Clearly, there is a sadness in these statements. Loneliness is one of the painful results of perfectionism. So is the thought of what might have been if perfectionists had had the courage to at least try to relate to others. All too often "the three favorite phrases of the perfectionist are: 'could have,' 'should have,' 'would have.' If you are living in this emotional state, the official state song is 'If Only.' Always standing on tiptoe, always reaching, stretching, trying, but never making it."[8] One pays a terrible price for such impossibly high goals.

Eugene O'Neill's play *Desire Under the Elms* centers on the character of Ephraim Cabot, a closefisted, greedy, self-righteous hypocrite. Through a series of tragedies, the play ends with Ephraim Cabot left alone on his farm. As the sheriff leaves him by himself, Ephraim comments that it is the best farm in the county, a place anyone would want to own. It may have been the best farm around, but it was probably the loneliest place around as well. Cabot's unrealistic goals, which he set for himself and for his family, led to the death of his wife and to nothing but hatred and rejection from his sons. He was left in a lonely world of unrealistic expectations.

Setting unrealistic or extremely high goals does not ensure success. This was found to be true in a study conducted by David Burns. He met with a group of thirty-four highly successful insurance agents and asked them to score themselves on his Perfectionism Scale. He found that in the group, eighteen identified themselves as clearly being perfectionists; the other sixteen considered themselves to be nonperfectionistic. Before meeting with the group, Burns predicted that the perfectionists, who probably set higher goals for themselves, would have the higher incomes. Instead, he found that the perfectionists earned an average of $15,000 less per year than the nonperfectionists. Other studies have shown that top athletes have an absence of perfectionistic thinking styles. Even the dropout phenomenon in graduate schools has been directly linked to perfectionistic thinking styles.[9] Students would rather drop out of a graduate program than not be the most successful in the class.

It appears that "while a healthy achiever rates only her performance, the perfectionist is really rating herself."[10] Of course, when the results are in, this person will always come up short. Everyone may rave about her meal, but if she sees a spot on a glass, the party is ruined. Or she may leave a job interview feeling that she was a failure because she didn't handle it perfectly—even though she got the job. Here the dichotomous thinking patterns of Maximizing and Minimizing interact with unrealistic goals, perpetuating the perfectionistic way of life. The pleasure of the party guests is minimized while the spot on the glass is maximized. Or the joy of getting the job is minimized while the imperfect interview is maximized.

One perfectionist described the results of her unrealistic goals for herself like this:

With my husband I try to do *everything* right. My apologies over understandable mistakes are so intense they annoy him. With my friends, I find that I don't invite them over unless *everything* is in apple-pie order. I miss a lot of opportunities for enjoying my friends this way. I sometimes drive my coworkers crazy over some small point. I was told I spend too much time on nonessentials.

The pattern of perfectionistic thinking is seen at work within the business world in other ways. It is seen in performance reviews, which all too often minimize employees' strengths and maximize their weaknesses. Workers are usually compared with some idealized image of how they should be, and they always come up short. In the same way, one of the most commonly mentioned problems in organizations that manage by objectives "is the difficulty in writing *realistic* quantitative objectives. There is a fear on the part of management to adjust their objectives to reality."[11]

In the area of consumerism, perfectionism is at work. Advertising is aimed at portraying the image of perfection. People buy according to this image, not according to reality—whether they can afford it or not, of course. Women are especially prone to buying clothes according to how they imagine themselves to be, not how they really are. People buy products with a concern for projecting an idealized self-image that they imagine is desirable to others.[12] The middle-aged man buying a red Porsche is trying to project an image that he thinks is desirable to others, regardless of how he measures up in reality. He doesn't want to consider that aspect. If our culture says that the ideal is to be a certain way, many people quickly decide to spend the money in order to be that way. The resulting hollowness is related to the third characteristic of perfectionistic thinking— lowered self-esteem. If a man is trying to project a certain image with a red Porsche, it won't be long before he will need a red Ferrari to project that same image.

Self-esteem cannot be built through externals or through achievement.

LOWERED SELF-ESTEEM

This third characteristic of perfectionists is just as pervasive as the other two. If goals for performance are unrealistic and perfectionists think in terms of all-or-nothing, the failure to meet these impossible goals is bound to result in lowered self-esteem. This sets in motion a cycle that leads to the misplaced belief that self-worth can be measured *only* in terms of accomplishments. Suzanne McNear writes, "We must be perfect, if we are to be loved or even liked, and since we know we ultimately will fall short of this standard, we're terrified that other people will find us out."[13]

When asked how they feel when they cannot do something perfectly, perfectionists said:

- "You have just described the height of misery!"

- "I don't even start. I don't do it. I won't do it. It's too frustrating. I feel foolish and shameful when things are less than perfect."

- "I get frustrated and a little angry. Then I get a little sad and feel defeated."

- "I feel tense, down on myself, frustrated, angry."

- "I feel inadequate. I hurt inside. I'm afraid I won't be accepted."

With lowered self-esteem coupled with these types of negative feelings, the all-or-nothing thinking is perpetuated, and the tendency to set unrealistic goals is intensified. So the self-defeating cycle is continued, from misery to misery.

In *The Rime of the Ancient Mariner,* Samuel Taylor Coleridge portrayed an old seaman who told of the day he killed an albatross with his crossbow. His fellow crewmen felt that the bird was a sign of good luck and that, with its death, bad luck would follow them—and it did. The ship lay becalmed for days at the equator. The thirsty seamen blamed the Ancient Mariner for their plight and hung the dead albatross around his neck as a sign of his guilt. Although the old man confessed his misdeed and performed penance, he still suffered the agony of his guilt and felt compelled to tell his story again and again. His present was overshadowed by the guilt of his past. His future was dark, for he could not rid himself of his guilt. He could not accept his mistake and was obsessed with what he *should not have done.* Like a perfectionist, he believed that if he could just try harder, he could break free from his guilt.

A SELF-DESTRUCTIVE CYCLE

Individuals who try harder to make themselves and others live up to their expectations often end up excluding from their lives activities and people they would enjoy. But because they don't have the time or the energy to do the activity perfectly or develop the perfect relationship, they don't even try.

We've come full circle in our understanding of the world of the perfectionist. The all-or-nothing thinking leads to the setting of unrealistic goals that leads to lowered feelings of self-esteem when those goals cannot be met. The whole perfectionistic thinking pattern is a self-destructive cycle.

The cycle works like this: In attempting to deal with the need to control the dichotomies of either-or thinking, perfectionists encounter the hurdle effect, where all they can see are the problems up ahead, or they minimize past successes and maximize the risk of failure up ahead, or they attribute negative motives to other people. They see everything in terms of black and white, of all-or-nothing, so it stands to reason that any goals set will be a reflection of those dichotomies. Either they do it perfectly, or they don't do it at all. When they don't do it or fail to reach their impossible goals, they lower their opinion of themselves. Their attempts at trying harder are simply new unrealistic goals that cannot be met and lead to lowered self-esteem and unhappiness. "The answer to the less-than-perfect performance and the unpleasant emotional response is a resolution to try harder and 'be perfect' the next time."[14] This cycle is illustrated in figure 3.

In the event that an unrealistic goal is met, the cycle does not really change much. One would think that if perfectionists met an unrealistic goal, they would feel better about themselves, but as I have shown, the di-

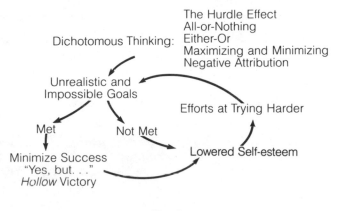

Fig. 3.

chotomous pattern of thinking will lead them to minimize their success, saying something like, "Yes, but I
should have done it sooner or more often," or something
to the effect of neutralizing the success. Their "hollow"
victory doesn't feel much different from other attempts
that failed. The result is the same—lowered self-
esteem.

There is an old adage that applies here: Trying
harder only gets you more of the same. It appears that
the "more of the same" for perfectionists is more guilt
and dissatisfaction, more frustration and shame. So
why do they persist? What keeps them caught in the
vicious cycle? Even in the face of evidence that aiming
for perfection does not result in a higher level of performance, perfectionists will not give up. It appears the
roots of perfectionism go even deeper, as we will see in
the next chapters.

CHAPTER THREE

The Problem with Being Average

*A man can do his best only by confidently seeking (and
perpetually missing) an unattainable perfection.*
—Ralph Barton Perry

*R*ecently, a highly successful woman was telling me
about a very painful memory of her childhood. She related an incident that took place when she was in the
fifth grade. The whole class had been given an intelligence test, and for some reason, the teacher was com-
menting to the class on the higher scores achieved by
some of the students. Driven by her curiosity, this
woman had been able to sneak a look at the results, and
to her *horror* (as she described it), she found that her IQ
was 100!

She was average! In fact, her score was exactly in the
middle, which meant that half the people taking the
test would score higher than her and half would score
lower. The knowledge that she was "average" humili-
ated her at that time and still does. Ever since that
event, she has considered herself to be stupid because
she only scored as average.

THE AVOIDANCE OF THE AVERAGE

My perfectionistic wife looked at this chapter and said, "I would be appalled and shocked if I had to be average in any way. I just can't accept that for me—death is better!" She understood exactly how that woman felt. So would another perfectionist, who said, "I try to remember that *average* isn't a dirty word."

When Jan and I surveyed a number of people on perfectionism, we found that 83 percent said they were dissatisfied if their performance was average. Being average in anything is apparently experienced as shameful—as something to be avoided at all cost. Or in Jan's words—death is better than being average! It seems that many people equate an average performance with a poor performance.

When we look in a dictionary for definitions of *average*, we find the most obvious mathematical. Other ideas suggested are *typical* and *usual*. *Webster's New Dictionary of Synonyms* lists as synonyms for *average*: *middling, medium, indifferent, moderate, mediocre, and second-rate*. Other synonyms are *fair, run-of-the-mill, so-so,* and *tolerable*.

This is an interesting mix of synonyms. *Middling* and *medium* apply to what is midway between extremes on a scale and would seem to imply a sufficiency as well as a lack of distinction. *Mediocre* implies a negative quality, which stresses the undistinguished aspects of what is average. *Indifferent* and other words on the list suggest a sense of inadequacy. Based upon these word associations, it is easy to see why being average is believed to be unacceptable or, at best, barely adequate.

I was surprised by this, so I looked up the word *imperfection* in *Roget's International Thesaurus*. To me, the word means something less than perfect, but certainly acceptable. But the synonyms included *defective, faulty, inadequate, deficient,* and *unsound.* The either-or thinking noted in the previous chapter is clearly seen here, where everything is viewed as either superlative or a dismal failure.

When we use positive-sounding terms such as *intelligent, good, sound, above average,* or *first-rate,* we seem to imply an absoluteness that we may not intend. In our educational process, we are taught that we

> **need not realize any of these positive qualities absolutely; that it is not in the nature of human beings to realize any such qualities absolutely; that it is normal for human beings to feel some degree of anxiety, fear, perplexity, or hostility; that it is normal to make some mistakes or be inefficient at times; and that having such limitations is human and normal and not a basis for self-condemnation.**[1]

But the exact opposite is taught by example and believed by our culture.

This aversion to the average infiltrates every area of our lives, not just in the way we define our words. A look through a magazine or an evening spent analyzing TV commercials will confirm the media's effect on our intolerance for anything less than perfect.

One of the most obvious ad campaigns that reflects this attitude is a series run by Dewar's Scotch. Each magazine ad presents a highly successful, perfectly groomed person, like the Wall Street attorney who sky dives, makes his own sushi, races a Porsche, is in perfect physical condition and, of course, drinks the advertiser's product. If someone like him, who obviously has achieved near perfection, buys Dewar's, shouldn't we?

Whatever we buy, it must be the best! Of course, we can't blame it all on the media. They are only appealing to our existing desire to be and to have the best. There is something inside us that drives us to search for the perfect in everything. Even our cartoons depict this concept. The proud eagle in "Tumbleweeds" knows how to meet this human expectation. (See Figure 4.)

We don't want average eagles any more than we want average relationships. We want the perfect marriage with the perfect partner. We also want to be perfect parents who raise perfect kids, who require nothing from us and do everything right. We search the bookshelves for anything that looks like it will help us in our quest.

Of course, that means we have to be perfect. We want perfect teeth, perfect skin, perfect weight, and perfect health. We dream of a family, a community, a country, and a world at peace—all in perfect harmony. No wonder we are repelled by the thought of anything

Fig. 4.

average. It certainly doesn't "sell." And it just as certainly resists being defined as a positive quality.

This whole discussion in "defense" of the average probably sounds mediocre to a perfectionist, in part because the average is defined in a *collective* sense. Perfectionists are appalled by the average because it means being lost in the crowd—it means not excelling. This is what bothered the woman I described at the beginning of this chapter about the results of her IQ test. This is what Jan was reacting to when she said she'd rather die than be average. Average results are compared and judged in relation to everyone else's results. That's why parents push their kids to excel in Little League, soccer, school activities, and grades. Parents want their children, when compared with other children, to be the best—or at least one of the best.

An alternative might be to think of the average in an individual sense. Rather than compare someone's performance with that of others, why not compare it with how the individual expected to perform? This would mean seeing the average as a positive quality, repre-

senting a form of balance *within* the individual. For example, I might decide in advance that a project needs only an average performance—I don't have to do my absolute best. In this specific task, I might be happy with a 50 percent result, when compared with my own standard of what a 100 percent result might be. In chapter 9, there is a chart to help in the development of this approach. Each person's average will be different. In fact, depending on ability, the amount of time available, the importance of the task, and the circumstances, an individual's average could even vary.

There is very little help available to present the average in a positive way. Positive qualities are defined in absolute terms. An afternoon looking through self-help books in the library will demonstrate that "most of the writers [emphasize] only the positive qualities they see as constituting health and say nothing about what limitations would still be consistent with being psychologically healthy."[2] The impression given is that the healthy personality possesses certain positive qualities and anything less than that constitutes an unhealthy personality. A "healthy range" is not defined.

The result is that when perfectionists read that a

healthy personality is competent, intelligent, successful, unselfish, responsible, able to feel emotions, and so on, they take these traits and believe that the only way to be healthy is to possess them all in an absolute sense. Again, all-or-nothing thinking comes into play, forcing the pendulum to swing to the "all" side or to the "nothing" side. No "average" between the two is acceptable.

THE PROMISE OF PERFECTIONISM

The promise of perfectionism is basically a lie. It says that things can be perfect even though all the evidence indicates the exact opposite. The lie is based on the fact that when people are faced with the choice between what is *possible* and what is *desirable,* they usually choose what is desirable, whether it is possible or not. Paul Watzlawick notes that once individuals make the choice for the desirable, they usually make the "typical charges of mediocrity, callousness or inhumanity . . . at the advocates of the possible."[3] He quotes Richard Aubrey as saying, "While we pursue the unattainable, we make it impossible to achieve the realizable."[4]

Another danger in the lie of perfectionism is that perfectionism has a peculiar tendency to "somersault into its opposite and become the justification for the worst atrocities and the most inhuman repression that have blighted the history of mankind."[5] Hitler's holocaust was built on the desire to create the "perfect" human race. Religious fanatics have led armies enlisted for the purpose of purifying and "perfecting" the faith. Watzlawick adds that

> **the logic of the fanatic is of seductive simplicity. The radical believes he has gone to the roots, found the ultimate answer, the truth, or the real meaning of life, and this obligates him to change the world accordingly, no matter if the world wants to be or how absurd his "truth" may be.**[6]

The avoidance of the average can lead into another problem—that of being motivated more by the avoidance of the imperfect than of being motivated by the desire for the best. Individuals no longer strive for the best; they simply strive for the purpose of avoiding the imperfect. Instead of wanting to be good employees or some of the best in the company, perfectionists worry so much about being perceived as less than perfect that they make themselves ill over a small mistake. One perfectionist said, "I feel my perfectionism creeping up on me whenever I am under stress at work. I'm sure that my neck and shoulder pains have a lot to do with the amount of pressure I place on myself, sweating the small things."

Seen this way, perfectionism can become a form of self-punishment. Because goals are unrealistic, perfectionists experience the inevitable failure, followed by feelings of guilt and shame over that failure. When this happens, they have allowed the pendulum to swing to its extremes of all-or-nothing. The fear of failure rather than the desire for success lies at the root of motivation and behavior.

The irony is that the demand for a flawless performance can never be satisfied. It is like aiming for 11 on a scale of 10. A perfectionist said, "My drivenness has never allowed me to feel good about any performance, either mine or someone else's." This can be especially true of career-oriented women. All too often the message to these women is very clear: The only way to the top of the ladder for a woman is to do the job perfectly. There seems to be an abundance of superwomen in today's business world, but in contrast to the few who achieve the top, countless others are casualties of their perfectionism.

But there seems to be something more than an aversion to the average, the influence of the media, or the demands of the work place that pushes people to reach for the top. If the extreme swings of the pendulum to either perfection or imperfection are unsatisfactory, and the in-between of the average is offensive, there must be an alternative.

THE DRIVE FOR EXCELLENCE

A number of books out now suggest that the alternative to accepting the average or striving for perfectionism is pursuing excellence. That word—*excellence*—touches a button in each individual. In their book *In Search of Excellence*, Thomas Peters and Robert Waterman quote psychologist Ernest Becker, who "argues that man is driven by an essential 'dualism'; he needs both to be a part of something and to stick out. He needs at one and the same time to be a conforming member of a winning team and to be a star in his own right."[7] Becker speaks directly about the tendency to avoid the average. Everyone wants to play on the team but also dreams of hitting the game-winning home run.

In describing this conflicting desire, Becker notes: "Society . . . is a vehicle for earthly heroism. . . . Man transcends death by finding meaning for his life. . . . It is the burning desire for the creature to count. . . . What man really fears is not so much extinction, but extinction with *insignificance*."[8] Everyone wants to make a difference. Who has not thought or said, "I just want to make some kind of mark in history to say, 'I've been here'"?

It's this drive to make a mark that causes the child to get the correct answer in math class. It is the same thing that motivates the developing concert pianist to get every note correct. It's the chord that was struck within each of us as we watched Nadia Comaneci perform in the 1976 Olympics and achieve what then seemed impossible—a perfect score of 10. It's also at the root of every perfectionist's compulsive drive for perfection.

Karen Horney called this drive for the top the "search for glory." The search is "born from compelling inner necessities" and is a creative process. "Although destructive in its consequences, it nevertheless stems from man's best desires—to expand beyond his narrow confines."[9] Crossing over from the healthy aspects of this striving to the paralyzing effects of perfectionism is usually a subtle shift. One may have only a vague sense of making great demands on the self, for the demands are usually seen as genuine ideals. This person makes strenuous efforts to measure up to standards by fulfilling duties and obligations meticulously, but soon this need extends into every area of life and the demand becomes a *flawless* standard in the whole of life.

Eventually, such people attempt to master and control life through perfectionism. Perfectionists can actually feel superior because of their high standards. Their own sense of fairness, justice, and duty leads them to believe that everyone should act as they do. And then as if to show everyone, their success becomes the proof of their virtue. Conversely, any form of failure is proof of their lack of virtue and can be quite shattering.

This subtle shift from excellence to perfectionism can often be difficult for individuals to spot in themselves. It is even difficult to see in others.

It is difficult, but important, to draw the line between high standards of performance and perfectionism. Perfectionism goes beyond a healthy pursuit of excellence. Achievers strive for quality and genuinely enjoy the satisfaction of a job well done. Perfectionists compulsively demand only flawless performance and are really never satisfied and never finished.[10]

Steve Jobs, founder of Apple Computers, illustrates the danger of crossing this fine line. He founded an extremely successful company, representing what creativity and the drive for excellence can accomplish. But he is seen by many in the computer industry as "an immature person driven to extremes by his vision."[11] His extremes resulted in his company going on without him. The joy of doing a task gave way to the fear of not doing it perfectly. "Fear of failure, not desire for success, became the motivation."[12]

People seeking excellence strive for quality and still seem to genuinely enjoy the satisfaction of a job well done. They can rely on their own self-discipline to help them know that even when their best could not be "good enough," it had to be "enough." Joseph Cooke notes, "When I talk about perfectionism, it is not this reaching out, this pressing forward to a higher goal that I am referring to. Such striving is absolutely essential to growth. What I refer to is that attitude that makes perfection the prerequisite for acceptance."[13] True seekers of excellence live in tune with their objectives, seeking reasonable achievements through agreed-on objectives for both themselves and their subordinates.

Having a passion for excellence is good,

as long as we're not blocking ourselves or driving others away; as long as we make our standards work *for* us. . . . We're right to insist on quality, on aiming for greatness in the arts, in

science, in sports, in any field. . . . High standards need not be terrifying. The pursuit of excellence may mean that you will learn to cook a superb dinner instead of a mediocre one, that I will spend enough hours on the tennis court next year to become a good player instead of a poor one, that either one of us may put in that vital, productive extra hour at work instead of being the first out the door.[14]

Figure 5 shows the differences between the pursuit of excellence and the drive for perfectionism.

The pursuit of excellence is vastly different from the enslavement perfectionists experience in holding fast to their impossible dreams. But it is easy to cross over the fine line that separates the two, for "there is a sense in which the world is designed to extract every ounce of potential from us. We place similar demands within ourselves. Motivated by internal and external forces, we run to win. But we must be cautious. The legitimate desire for excellence can easily drive us to excess,"[15] especially the excess of perfectionism.

THE FINE LINE BETWEEN

works for me | works against me

EXCELLENCE | **PERFECTIONISM**
"Genuine striving"—personal best | Striving for "the ideal"

OUTLOOK	
Realistic: "It is . . ."	Idealistic: "It should be . . ."
STRIVING FOR	
The possible—accepts the possible	The impossible—desires the perfect
SELF-TALK	
I want . . .	I must . . .
I wish . . . **IS**	I should . . .
I would like . . .	I ought to . . .
STATED AS	
A request or desire	Always a demand
MOTIVATION	
Striving for positive	Avoidance of negative
Desire for success	Fear of failure
FOCUS ON	
Process	Product
POSITION IS	
Free . . . in pursuit of excellence	Slave . . . in prison of perfectionism
EXPECTS	
Best of self	Best in comparison to everyone else
LIFE VIEWED AS	
Challenge that is welcomed	Curse that is dreaded
RESULTS	
1. Accomplishment	1. Disappointment
2. Acceptance	2. Condemnation
3. Fulfillment	3. Frustration
4. Success	4. Failure
LIVE IN	
Reality	Fantasy
Real world	Unreal world
BOTTOM LINE	
THE TRUTH:	A LIE:
People and things do *not* have the ability to be perfect.	People and things have the ability to be perfect.

Fig. 5.

The Making of a Perfectionist

> *It's great to be great, but it's*
> *greater to be human.*
> *—Will Rogers*

*T*he aversion to being average emerges from the need within each of us as we work to grow to our full potential. There is a universal drive within that pushes us and gives us the feeling that anything is possible—we are omnipotent. This desire appears to be part of the human condition—it is still there within us, regardless of personality factors or family backgrounds.

By the time we become adults, most of us are quite good at either blocking out or hiding these feelings of omnipotence. But there is a period in childhood when these feelings are most obvious. We call it the *terrible twos*. During this stage of development, children act as if and believe that the world is their oyster. They seem to be almost intoxicated with their new awareness of the world, especially since they each seem to think that the world revolves around them. A big part of the joy of this stage is the awareness that a child has about self, the perception of being an autonomous self.

THE DEVELOPMENT OF DEFENSES

The powerful euphoria a child experiences during this period is interrupted now and then with the recognition that a parent is not present or is unavailable to meet every need. It's obvious to us as adults that a parent cannot be available to meet *every* need experienced by a child all of the time. When the parent is unavailable, the child may experience this as a feeling of helplessness, as shame at needing someone else, or simply as a very basic anxiety that comes from living in what is perceived as a hostile environment. In response to these unpleasant feelings, the child begins to build defenses into the personality that are designed as protection against such negative experiences.

Karen Horney said that this basic feeling of anxiety is based on "an insidiously increasing, all pervading feeling of being isolated and helpless in a potentially hostile world."[1] This is the same feeling that adults experience, especially when under stress. The way a child handles this anxiety early in life can be one of the major roots of perfectionism in adulthood.

Horney noted that this basic anxiety has three aspects—a feeling of isolation, a sense of helplessness, and the presence of hostility. When anxiety first occurs in early childhood, the child

61

feels the environment as a menace to his entire development and to his most legitimate wishes and strivings. He feels in danger of his individuality being obliterated, his freedom taken away, his happiness prevented. In an environment in which basic anxiety develops, the child's free use of energies is thwarted, his self-esteem and self-reliance is undermined, fear is instilled by intimidation and isolation, his expansiveness is warped through brutality—and the child is rendered helpless to defend himself adequately.[2]

This may be true in reality or only based on the child's perceptions.

Horney's description may sound like an extreme example of an anxious childhood, but it is not out of the ordinary. Many people I counsel tell me of childhood experiences of extreme rejection, cold hostility, and cruel brutality. One woman told me how her mother used a metal towel rack to hit her when she failed to follow through on any small detail while baby-sitting her younger siblings. When her older brother raped her, her mother laughed at her, believing the brother's protestations of innocence. The extreme pain of her childhood was directly related to her perfectionism in adulthood—for her to be anything less than perfect meant the possibility of more pain.

Often a parent will use a child for personal needs. In such cases the needs of the child are secondary to those of the parent. The woman mentioned above was expected to be the mother to her brothers and sisters because her mother didn't have time to be a mother or didn't want to be because of her own social life. Sometimes a parent will be so aloof from the parenting role that a child experiences a cold, unpredictable, and even dangerous environment. When a child has these types of early experiences, the *conditions* for perfectionism are already set in motion.

The important point to see, though, is that a child doesn't have to have an extremely negative experience, like this woman's experience, to feel anxiety. Crying alone and hungry in a crib will create anxiety in an infant. Perceptions of experiences determine the effect of those experiences. Just as a striving for glory is a common experience for all human beings, so is the experience of anxiety within the infant.

Out of necessity, the child seeks to alleviate these feelings of anxiety. Often the child will attempt to go back to that "omnipotent" stage of the twos and concentrate perfection and power upon the self. In doing this, the child attributes all his or her imperfections to the world outside the self and assigns the ideal to the self. Some theorists, including psychologist Althea Horner, believe that this idealizing of the self is a natural stage of development when the child "recognizes more fully the separateness of mother and the relative helplessness of the self."[3] Gradually over time the imagination sets to work and fashions within the child's mind an idealized picture of the self.

REAL SELF VERSUS IDEAL SELF

An example of this process of idealizing the self would be the cartoon that shows a grossly overweight, unkempt person standing in front of a mirror that has a reflection of a beautiful, meticulously groomed, thin person. In the cartoon, it is easy to see which is the real person and which is the idealized image of that person. When the mirror is in the mind, the distinction between the real and the ideal becomes too easily blurred, and over a period of time, the person actually begins to believe that the image in the mirror is the real self. There is no anxiety experienced by this idealized self because in the imagination the self is able to do everything perfectly. People with this idealized perception have accepted what they think they can become—the idealized self; thus, they no longer work to develop the real self. "They attempt to create the illusion that their actual self-representation is imbued with idealized qualities that will protect it from the experience of any frustration and against the imagined consequence of their rage in response to frustration."[4] In other words, in terms of our cartoon, the self that is outside the mirror looking at the reflection ceases to exist, and the only "reality" left is the image in the mirror.

We can look at the development of the ideal self as a twofold event. First, it is a typical result of how the individual copes with the normal feelings of anxiety during early development. Second, it marks the beginnings of perfectionistic trends and behaviors within the

Fig. 6.

individual. This second aspect is the result of the shifting of energy away from the development of the real self to the development of the ideal.

The true perfectionist will eventually direct *all* energies toward the *full* development of the ideal self. It is not just a touch-up job—the individual seeks a *total* transformation. Flawless beauty means there is no unwanted hair growth, no clogged pores, no scars from acne, no out-of-proportioned facial features, no unwanted fat or cellulite anywhere on the body. A "perfect" ad campaign means that every viewer of the TV commercial will be impressed by the product.

Most people come to the realization that these absolutes don't exist in life. For the perfectionist, however, the absolutes are a way of life. The degree of perfectionism in each person is a reflection of how much energy is directed toward the development of the ideal to avoid the feeling of anxiety.

Horney said that the individual tries "to achieve this goal by a complicated system of shoulds and taboos."[5] She pointed out that the perfectionist is different from Pygmalion, who tried to make another person into a creature of charm and beauty. The perfectionist

holds before his soul his image of perfection and unconsciously tells himself: "Forget about the disgraceful creature you actually *are;* this is how you *should* be; and to be this idealized self is all that matters. You should be able to endure everything, to understand

everything, to like everybody, to be always productive"—to mention only a few of these inner dictates.[6]

As I have said earlier, the scope of these dictates or demands on the self can cover every aspect of life or only certain areas. One should be totally honest or generous or self-sacrificing—or all three. One should be the perfect child, the perfect lover, the perfect spouse, the perfect parent, the perfect friend. One should not be fazed by anything; one's feelings should never be hurt. One should be spontaneous, yet always under perfect control. One should, should, should . . . ! Perfectionists place demands upon themselves that take over their lives because they are consumed by these "shoulds." One perfectionist described these feelings:

I saw my father as very successful in business. My older brother was very, very successful in college and in the navy. I felt I *had* to do well, too, like doctors' sons should be smart and become doctors, also. I tried extremely hard to *excel* at something so I could be "successful," too.

If we could get perfectionists to enumerate the list of demands or "shoulds" they make upon themselves, they would probably not be surprised. They might agree that the list is too difficult for anyone to achieve, but they would be quick to add that it is better to expect too much than too little. One perfectionist said:

I can remember as a child that everything had to be _perfect_ before I went to bed. I wanted my closet door shut, everything straight on my dresser, the curtains closed just right—they couldn't overlap. My bedspread had to be folded back just right. I couldn't relax and go to sleep if everything wasn't just perfect. I still can't!

A man who told how he was a perfectionist in only one area of his life said:

I can clearly recall in high school being obsessed with having my appearance be impeccable. I stayed up late nearly every night ironing my shirt and slacks for the next day. I could do it better than my mother—no kidding! I still can.

These areas of perfectionism may be a pervasive theme throughout one's life, or they may change based on the person's needs at any given period of time. Someone who may have wanted to be at the top of the class during school years may be just as compulsively driven to make the most money or to live in the nicest house in town. These ambitions can drive people to the point that they lose sight of what they are trying to do—the content or purpose of their behavior—and begin to focus more and more on the need to be Number One. What counts now to them is not what they do, but excelling in and of itself.

A woman described to me how she has been perfectionistic in the area of relationships. Every relationship has had to be harmonious—no problems, no hard feelings, no misunderstandings. She has often gone to great lengths to make certain that everyone around her is feeling good. Sometimes she drives her husband up the wall as she continually monitors how he is feeling about something. And of course, he has to have perfectly good feelings about whatever it is.

As we explored her behavior in this area, she began to see how her concern for everyone else was really a way to keep from being aware of whatever she was feeling in the situation. She ignored what her real self felt, all in the interest of being her ideal—a person who really cares about everyone else's feelings. Not only did she ignore her own needs, but she ended up overlooking what was really in the best interests of the other people around her, sometimes even to the point that she played the role of the martyr. When we talked about some of the roots of her behavior, she had great difficulty identifying how it began. She was willing to sacrifice her real self for some phantom of reality for reasons she could no longer identify.

This pattern of disregarding self to meet some standard can be quite extreme. Horney told of "an ambitious girl, aged ten, who thought she would rather be blind than not become the first in her class."[7] How tragic to sacrifice oneself for an often meaningless goal, and even sometimes for an impossible objective! A perfectionist told about herself in high school:

I attempted suicide because I was in a bind. I felt that I had done nothing worthwhile in my life, and I couldn't find any answer for my future. So I decided to end my life. I'd rather have been dead than not be perfect. I still feel that if I loosen up I will become second-rate.

The compulsiveness of perfectionism can also become an insatiable drive. There can be a sense of elation when a task is done well or even a hairsbreadth away from perfect. But the feeling never lasts. It cannot last, for it is a striving to make real something that exists only in the imagination. That's why so many perfectionists find out later that their drive to the top only leaves them more and more unsatisfied. When the real self has been buried beneath the false image of the ideal self, nothing can ever really satisfy. One must make more money, achieve more prestige, win more victories, conquer more tasks—all without a lasting feeling of satisfaction.

This will inevitably lead to constant terror over the possibility of failure. Some describe it as *the imposter complex*—the constantly nagging fear that others will find out that one is really a failure hiding behind a facade of success. A successful, perfectly dressed mortgage broker told me that not a day went by that he wasn't overwhelmed with the fear that the people he worked with would find out he was a phony. He's the one who used the term *the imposter complex* with me.

He found that the more he sought to bury the real self and develop the ideal of what he should be, the more intense were his reactions to frustration along the way. Panic, despair, depression, or rage can overwhelm someone when the possibility of failure raises its ugly head. Another perfectionist said, "Because I have such strong ideals about what I should be like, I can't objectively evaluate what I am like."

Once an individual has accepted the idealized self as reality, it becomes increasingly easy to lose a sense of reality about everything else. It becomes difficult to effectively evaluate even the small things in life. One perfectionist said that she contemplated for a week, in fear, the task of repainting a wooden drum set—a task that ended up taking ten minutes. A person can't be unrealistic about the self and still be realistic about the rest of life.

This mixing of the imagined with the real keeps perfectionists striving to reach the impossible. The goals and ideals held by these individuals have no checks and balances to keep them rooted in reality. In fact, they must often disregard reality to maintain the idealized image of the self.

Why would anyone seek to develop such a lifestyle? No one does it by design—it starts out as a way to avoid the anxiety of life. It starts as a way to control life, not to destroy the real self. In exchange for protection from fear and anxiety, the price is self-deception. The individual tends to project personal standards on others and looks down on them for not measuring up. The individual's self-condemnation is externalized, which serves to perpetuate the deception of the self.

Of course there are positive values experienced along the way or else the cycle would be easy to identify and break. Many perfectionists find meaning in their lives by the pursuit of the impossible. Some are even energized when faced with the challenge of the impossible, although the energy is eventually dissipated because of frustration and disappointment. Others find that the cycle is maintained as part of a family tradition.

THE FAMILY FACTOR

When we asked our group of perfectionists to name the other perfectionists in their families, 44 percent said the father only, 32 percent said both father and mother, and 8 percent said the mother only. The other 16 percent said they developed their perfectionism even though no one else in the family was perfectionistic.

Those who identified the father as the perfectionist attested to his strong influence. Here are some of the comments about these dads:

- "Meticulous in his appearance, highly disciplined in his actions, and very demanding of all of us to be the same."

- "Nothing was ever done well enough for Dad, never done right, never complete enough."

- "Dad made sure we had an absolutely spotless home and car. No arguments were allowed, no risks were taken, no competitive sports encouraged. Mistakes were criticized openly and often."

- "My dad drove himself in everything he did. He would redo, rework until it was right. He died at 47 of a heart attack."

When the mother entered the picture, she was often seen as competing with the father. One person noted that "Mom failed as a career homemaker, and instead turned with a vengeance to business for achievement and self-validation."

Often the child picked up these traits from the parent and took them to new levels of perfectionism. Or if the child adopted the values of the perfectionistic parent, the other parent would attempt in vain to dissuade the child from perfectionism. One person said that if she "wanted Knudson's Yogurt, and we had Johnston's—I would have none. My mother continually said to me, 'You have to learn to make do' and 'You must learn to be flexible.'"

A person who noted how the expectations of the parent were internalized said, "I was comfortable with Father's expectations, since my basic aims were to do well." But others noted that their perfectionism came from the desire to be accepted by the parent. One person said, "My dad had the expectations. I was afraid of him, and I didn't know why he didn't like me. I couldn't figure out what I had to do to make him like me. I just knew I couldn't do it right, but I kept trying."

A common experience involved grades. One individual commented, "If I got a 98 on a paper, Daddy would say, 'Why didn't you get 100?'" Another respondent said that once she got an $A-$ when all her other grades were A's. Both parents looked at the report card, and their only comment was, "What are you going to do about this $A-$?" She added, "For years, I thought all families had these expectations and standards."

Perfectionists often had highly critical parents who doled out love and approval in exchange for achievement. This problem is compounded by what we noted in the last chapter, which is the inability of our language to indicate any degree of quality, short of perfection, that is acceptable. Both parents, along with other significant people in the child's life, encourage the development of the ideal self.

One of the responses on the survey noted:

When I was in the fifth grade, my teacher often ridiculed me in front of the entire class if my assignment was less than perfect. She would say that I was lazy and that the work wasn't worthy of me. The other kids would laugh, and I lived in fear that entire year. She was probably trying to motivate me, but I hated her. She gave me straight A's on my report cards, but was never happy if I didn't live up to her standard *all the time.*

Instead of motivating behavior, perfectionism seems to be associated with behavioral problems in school. In one study, perfectionism showed up as one of eight factors associated with behavior problems. In addition:

Children rated as depressed by their parents on the Personality Inventory for Children evidenced significantly more conduct problems, anxiety, impulsive hyperactivity, learning problems, psychosomatic problems, *perfectionism*, [emphasis added] and muscular tension at home than children rated as nondepressed.[8]

Throughout American history, children have been thought of as seeds to be cultivated by parents, all for the purpose of some larger goal or purpose. When this goal is to fulfill some perfectionistic needs within the parents, however, the child is in trouble. Parental worship of success deprives the child of personal needs, especially the need for self-direction. The child takes on the goals of the parents, which are usually impossibly perfectionistic. In addition, the child's goals are derived from the parents' own frustrations and have nothing to do with the child's interests or abilities. But the child, as we have seen, often internalizes the goals of the parents and becomes a taskmaster.

We have observed that perfectionism can be fostered within the family by a spirit of criticism, through the observation of parents' expectations of themselves, and through the setting of extremely high standards by the parents or significant others. A fourth situation can set the child up for perfectionism, and that is the lack of clear standards being set within the home. One perfectionist noted that at age seven, she had to "nag" her family to get the things she needed to organize her room. Another told how she used to put lists of things to be done on her mom's bedroom door to help her mom get organized. Her behavior was a reflection of her need for clear standards.

Another factor that seems to encourage the perfectionism cycle is the occasional reward or payoff. One person wrote, "I always liked the attention and strokes my successes brought. It was euphoric to succeed and really feel that I was on top of the world." It was only later that the frustration would come back because of the inability to remain "on top of the world" through performance or achievement.

What starts as a process to avoid fears and anxieties in childhood is reinforced by family and culture during growth. During the adolescent period, the person has the opportunity to work through some of the unfinished tasks of childhood. If these are not completed, the patterns of childhood can become firmly entrenched by adulthood. Understanding its roots can weaken the hold of perfectionism, but there's still one other area to consider that often lies at the base of perfectionism.

CHAPTER · FIVE

The Ultimate Fantasy

> *The desires of men are insatiable. In Eden,*
> *there emerged a desire to become perfect*
> *and establish equality with God.*
> —*Jeremy Bentham*

We have seen that each of us has an internal drive for glory that pushes us to achieve. The same drive pushes many people into the area of perfectionism. This drive can be traced back to Adam and Eve. While they were in the Garden of Eden, all their needs were met; yet, there emerged within them the desire to be perfect and to establish equality with God. The serpent appealed to this desire when he said, "God knows that in the day you eat of it [the fruit of the tree] your eyes will be opened, and you will be like God" (Gen. 3:5). Built into the human self, almost from the very beginning, were the jealousy of God's perfection and the desire to be like him.

Several chapters later in Genesis, it is recorded that men came together in a combined effort to construct a tower directly to the heavens in order to "make a name" for themselves (see 11:4). Because we do not have the courage to be imperfect, we strive to be like God—to be perfect. There is a thin line

> **between admiration (or worship) of the Deity and jealousy of Him, between the hunger to be *like* God and the hunger to *be* God. Religion seeks in holiness an antidote to sin and evil; irreligion seeks in superhumanness an antidote to God. In the pit of the human heart lies a seed of rivalry with God,[1]**

which began in the Garden of Eden and is reaffirmed within each of us. We participate in the rebellion of Satan, who was the first to say, "I will be like the Most High" (Isa. 14:14).

This haunting desire to be like God is motivated by our pride and by our need to be self-sufficient. "We would each like to be so perfect that it would not have been necessary for God to have created anyone else, nor ultimately for there to have been a God at all. In the frustration of our human impotence, we dream of being omnipotent."[2] We would seldom be so bold as to tell anyone of this dream—we simply reveal it in our drive for perfection.

HUMANKIND IN A BIND

Either-or, all-or-nothing dichotomous thinking places us in a bind. For most of us, it is obvious that we cannot be God. We intellectually can agree that we cannot be perfect. But we don't want to face the awful anxiety of being human. Just as the devil tempted Eve in the garden, so he tempts each of us with the offer of unlimited powers. Like Faust, we are offered the "devil's pact," where one can obtain omnipotent powers on the condition of selling one's soul and going to hell. We are all susceptible to that temptation because it represents an easy way to omnipotence.

The temptation is not as clearly spoken to us as it was to Eve, but the deal is the same. We think we can become like God, who is all-good. Instead, as Horney stated, "man in reaching for the Infinite and Absolute also starts destroying himself."[3] She also noted, "Speaking in these symbolic terms, the easy way to infinite glory is inevitably also the way to an inner hell of self-contempt and self-torment."[4] Unable to be like God—all-good—we end up being all-bad, which is intolerable. One of the defense systems we use to handle this bind is called *splitting*. Since we are *either* all-good *or* all-bad, we need to split off the part of us that seems bad. Adam did this very quickly in the garden when he told God, "The woman whom You gave to be with me, she gave me of the tree, and I ate" (Gen. 3:12). In other words, he was saying, "It's Your fault, God—it's that woman *You gave me.*" He took the bad part of himself and projected it on Eve and on God!

But Eve was not to be outdone. She quickly followed suit when she responded to God's question: "The serpent deceived me, and I ate" (Gen. 3:13). Her defense went along these lines: "I'm bad only because of the serpent, which by the way, God, You created. Therefore, I'm not really bad—it's someone else's fault."

The perfectionistic thought pattern follows the same route when things are less than perfect. Pass the blame! "It's her fault!" "He took all my time!" "The boss gave me something else to do, and I never got to it." "I've just been too busy." One of the best defenses against the lack of perfection is to blame someone else. As Solomon said, "There is nothing new under the sun" (Eccles. 1:9).

The blame game never works. It didn't help Adam and Eve then, and it doesn't help human beings now. Perfectionists are left with the tendency to think of themselves as all-bad. The individual develops

an attitude that says, in effect, "I cannot accept myself if I in any way fall short of perfection." And along with this attitude is the crippling conviction that other people will not accept me when I fall short. And behind all is the dreadful feeling that God will not accept me. He may indeed be willing to save me from hell, but only at the cost of wiping out nearly everything that is really me. Meanwhile . . . He finds me little better than a nasty, dirty object. I am so far from perfection that almost everything I am and do displeases Him.[5]

Perfectionists believe themselves to be identified with God through Christ for the purpose of salvation, but from that point on, they must prove themselves acceptable.

Of course, perfectionists deny this in their theology. Like Paul, they preach a theology of grace, but that grace applies only to the act of salvation, not to the process of everyday life. I see this all too often in people seeking counseling. Their relationship with God is based on how well they perform. They are drawn to faith in God by an awareness of their "badness," but the day-to-day solution to their "badness" is to try harder and to do things perfectly.

One man is so overwhelmed by his sense of badness that he moves from church to church because he is certain that he let down someone and needs to start over somewhere else. He comes to therapy for a while until he is convinced within himself that I think he is awful, and then he stays away until he feels so desperate that he must come back. Sure, he knows that God accepts him on the basis of faith and grace, but that's just the beginning. He must now prove that he is worthy of that grace. He must perform in a perfect way. But no matter how well he does, his past is simply too awful, and he just can't see how he can make up for it with God.

Another person I know is caught up in the "reward" that *must* be worked for. She thinks that from the point of salvation, God starts keeping score. Those with the highest scores will get the biggest rewards, so she must perform, perform, perform. She works full-time in her job, works full-time in her church, and berates herself for not doing enough.

Another approach is that of individuals who construct a very thorough list of do's and don'ts to determine who is good and who is bad. They are susceptible to these codes of legalism because they think such codes can help control feelings of badness. Like the Pharisees of New Testament times, they add lists upon lists to cover every possible contingency. But the compiling and the following of such lists can make things worse: "If I can follow the lists, I can be good. But the more I follow the lists of laws, the more laws I need to cover all the contingencies, and the more I am confronted with my feelings of badness."

Some people control feelings of badness by comparing themselves to others who are more overtly "bad" than they are. This leads to feelings such as, "I have a corner on goodness. I'll be the only one in heaven." Not only do some churches foster this kind of thinking, but cults thrive on it. Cultists believe they have a special insight into truth: "If you will just join us and pursue our grandiose aims, you will be a good person." One doesn't have to go to the extreme of looking at the ruthlessly pursued ambitions of Nazi Germany to see how easily people can be led astray by these claims. The forms can be much more subtle: "You should come to our church, our pastor teaches the Bible the right way." "I can't stand going to this church, the people are too social." "Do what we tell you, and you'll find the right way to God."

When someone splits off the "bad" part of the self and projects it onto another person or denies its existence, the individual is actually alienating a part of the self; the individual is no longer whole. The nature of the split is such that the system maintains itself to avoid confronting reality, and one way to accomplish this is to stay among people who share similar views. The problem is that the individual never finds the real self or discovers all that God has planned.

Paul talked about this feeling of self-alienation in Romans 7. He struggled to do the good but kept getting confronted with his badness. He wrote, "I don't understand myself at all, for I really want to do what is right, but I can't. I do what I don't want to—what I hate. . . . It seems to be a fact of life that when I want to do what is right, I inevitably do what is wrong" (vv. 15, 21 TLB). He ended the chapter by saying, "Oh, what a terrible predicament I'm in!" (v. 24 TLB).

SELF-ACCEPTANCE OR SELF-PUNISHMENT

Paul knew the spiritual solution. Earlier he wrote, "But now God has shown us a different way to heaven—not by 'being good enough' and trying to keep his laws, but by a new way. . . . Now God says he will accept and acquit us—declare us 'not guilty'—if we trust Jesus Christ to take away our sins" (Rom. 3:21–22 TLB). He continued, "Then what can we boast about doing, to earn our salvation? Nothing at all. Why? Because our acquittal is not based on our good deeds; it is

based on what Christ has done and our faith in him"
(v. 27 TLB).

David Seamands, author and pastor, states that in
spite of these clear principles, "perfectionism is the
most disturbing emotional problem among evangelical
Christians. It walks into my office more than any other
single Christian hang-up."[6] It also walks into my office
with almost everyone I see. With it comes an oversen-
sitivity that includes a great scrupulosity and a legalism that is overconcerned with the externals of faith.
These people do not like themselves, and they are quite
certain that God shares the same opinion of them. They
insist on punishing themselves with a list of what Paul
called "regulations." Paul asked the Colossians, "Why
. . . do you subject yourselves to regulations—'Do not
touch, do not taste, do not handle . . .' ? These things
indeed have an appearance of wisdom in self-imposed
religion, false humility, and neglect of the body, but are
of no value against the indulgence of the flesh" (Col.
2:20-21, 23).

These kinds of people "become guilt-ridden, over-
loaded, tight-haloed, unhappy, and uncomfortably
yoked Christians. They are rigid in their outlook, frigid
in their lovelessness, conforming to the approval and
disapproval of others. Yet, paradoxically, they critically
judge, and blame, and bind those"[7] trying to do the
same thing. They do not live in reality—they are denying their real selves and trying to create a spiritually
ideal self. This spiritualizing somehow makes it seem
more noble, but the issue is the same—attempting to

split off the bad side, denying and disowning it, in a futile effort to prove that they are good.

Often I find that people's attempts to prove to God that they are good are really attempts to prove it to themselves. I tried to get a woman to understand this by pretending that she had asked me for $10,000 and that I had just given her a check for that amount. She put the "check" in her purse, and not only did she continue to ask me for the money, but she tried to prove to me that she was worthy of receiving it. But all the time she did this, she had the check in her purse, uncashed! There was obviously nothing to prove to me, for she had the money. In that situation, it was clear that she was trying to prove her worth to herself. She needed to simply accept the fact that she had the money.

The choice seems to be between accepting redemption or rejecting it and punishing the self in order to be worthy of redemption. When stated this way, it seems to be a clear choice, but the problem with simply accepting redemption is that the individual has to accept reality, which contains both good and bad. That is how God sees and accepts everyone—with goodness and badness all wrapped together. That's reality.

Basically, the choice can be seen in this way. On the one hand, I am trying to be God through my perfectionism. I fail to meet these standards, so I must punish myself by trying harder to do the impossible—that is, to be God. On the other hand, I recognize that I am like God, made in His image, only I am both good and bad. God accepts me this way; therefore I accept myself.

I don't have to be God; I can simply be human.

Paul wrote, "Therefore, having been justified by faith, we have peace with God through our Lord Jesus Christ. . . . And not only that, but we also glory in tribulations" (Rom. 5:1, 3). I think that the tribulations he mentioned include the awful anxiety we encounter when we face reality. But when we face this terrible experience and go through it, we find hope at the other end. It is a hope that does not disappoint, for Paul added that through Christ's "righteous act the free gift came to all men, resulting in justification of life" (Rom. 5:18).

It appears that many would want to accuse religious faith of being a cause of perfectionism in human beings. Perhaps such verses as Matthew 5:48 lead to such accusations: "Therefore you shall be perfect, as your Father in heaven is perfect." But to blame perfectionism on an injunction that can just as clearly refer to a refining process is to miss the whole point of faith. It is clear that imperfect human beings bring their perfectionistic tendencies to the spiritual realm and attempt to impose spiritual reasons for what is a typical human problem. As we will see later, the clear message of Jesus is that we are accepted just as we are, with all our imperfections and flaws. We are to resist the human tendency to seek acceptance and approval, especially in this case where God's acceptance and approval are already unconditionally there.

The Prison of Perfectionism

People with perfectionistic values are true children of our individualistic society.
—Brian L.

People pay a high price for their perfectionism. "Studies show that people who blight their lives with impossibly high goals are likeliest to suffer health problems, low self-esteem, troubled personal relationships, test anxiety, social anxiety, writer's block, decreased productivity, even depression."[1] No wonder 70 percent of the people we talked with said that perfectionists were less happy than other people; 30 percent thought they were about the same as others. It was interesting that no one felt happier being a perfectionist, but two respondents said that sometimes there was a brief sense of elation at a job done well.

When we asked perfectionists what it feels like when they can't do something perfectly, they said:

- "You have just described the height of misery!"

- "FRUSTRATION!"

- "I absolutely hate it."

- "I feel inadequate and actually hurt inside."

- "I get knots in my stomach and want to just give up."

- "I feel foolish and shameful."

- "I get frustrated, a little angry, and then a little sad and defeated."

- "I can't look back on anything I've done and feel proud and satisfied."

We noted in chapter 2 that perfectionists tend to earn less as well as perform at a lower standard over the long haul than nonperfectionists. One study noted that tendency in the form of accident proneness. The report focused on a flying accident by a young naval pilot in the final stages of his training. He was by his own admission a perfectionist, continuing a task until it was complete and perfect. If he failed to do anything perfectly, he became quite depressed and very compulsive in the next attempt. His training had added even more pressure to his already perfectionistic tendencies and contributed to the accident. The article noted that "with this in mind and considering his recent errors, he again may have been so channelized in not making a mistake that it stimulated error."[2] The obsession with doing a perfect job caused him to make a mistake.

In the events leading up to the accident, he underresponded to what the plane was doing and then, in seeking to correct that mistake, made what was called a slip of the hand. Like a slip of the tongue, the action taken by the pilot was consciously known to be incorrect, but subconsciously allowed to happen and then corrected. But the correction was not in time, and he and the instructor had to eject prior to the crash.

The perfectionism of the pilot in this case showed strong similarities to other reports of accidents. He clearly thought in dichotomies of all-or-nothing, believing he was either perfect or a total failure. He paradoxically refused to take any blame for his errors, claiming instead that he acted in "the way he was taught." He also showed an inattention to reality by his insistence on a perfect performance. When given another opportunity to fly, he repeated his earlier error, only this time the instructor was able to take control of the aircraft in time to avert a crash.

OBSESSIVE-COMPULSIVE BEHAVIOR

This young man's perfectionism worked against his dream of being a naval pilot. He was diagnosed as being obsessive-compulsive and disqualified from the program. For many people, their perfectionism becomes an obsession, sometimes leading to compulsive, repetitive behavior that has no meaning in reality, such as continual hand washing.

A study of hospitalized obsessive-compulsive patients in Bethesda, Maryland, found that "their families tend to keep to themselves. They tend to be overly meticulous, perfectionists, very proud of their own way of doing things."[3] The study found that the compulsive behavior, in most cases, was designed to act as a barrier against emotional closeness. Perfectionists who are working on the development of the ideal self, not the real self, usually do not want people too close, for the ideal self cannot relate very well.

Dr. Nathan Rickles identified from his counseling what he called the *angry woman syndrome*. These women

> **displayed periodic outbursts of unprovoked anger, marital maladjustment, serious suicide attempts, proneness to abuse of alcohol and drugs, a morbidly oriented critical attitude to people and a contrary obsessive need to excel in all endeavors, with an intense need for neatness and punctuality.[4]**

Their constant, obsessive drive for perfection proved to be their undoing. It was the root of their destructive anger.

All these obsessional habits begin in relation to anxiety and the attempt by the individual to avoid it. We saw in an earlier chapter how the development of the ideal self is basically an attempt to avoid the anxiety of childhood. These women have perceptions of such poor childhood experiences that they must at all costs avoid any anxiety. They learned early that if things could be perfect, there would be no anxiety. As a result, they become obsessed with perfection and appear to be highly successful. They cannot handle this success, however, because they cannot handle any criticism or competition without experiencing extreme rage. Their relationships are filled with chaos.

Freud thought that people developed obsessive behaviors because they were attempting to hide terrible feelings of anger, like the women described above. But training programs during the 1960s and '70s that urged people to let their anger out were rarely, if ever, successful in creating change. The repression of anger is neither the root of obsessive behavior nor the root of perfectionism.

More recent theorists, including Harry Stack Sullivan, have viewed perfectionism as a way of dealing with feelings of insecurity and uncertainty that result from growing up in an unloving household. . . . the problem is not the hostile impulses, but rather the need to be loved and accepted.[5]

Obsessive-compulsive behavior is another form of "trying harder"—an extreme form. Leadership studies show that perfectionism is a counterproductive attitude. William Criddle illustrates this in the chart shown in figure 7.[6]

The interesting thing about this chart is that a middle level of motivation results in the optimal perfor-

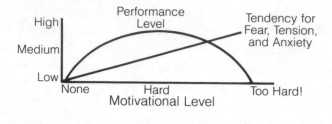

Fig. 7.

mance. Contrary to the thinking of the obsessive person, trying too hard decreases the level of performance, and it actually continues to raise the level of anxiety. In the same way, writers who try too hard to make every sentence perfect find that they write very little or none at all. Demanding that someone be perfectly creative is the same as demanding that someone *must* be spontaneous—which is a contradiction. No one can be spontaneous on demand.

Obsessive-compulsive people are not able to be spontaneous. In fact, they are not able to do much except talk about what they wish they could do. One woman complained that she hadn't taken a vacation for several years because she just "had too much to do." What she does is check and recheck all the details of her home and clean and reclean her kitchen.

She entertains, but it's not for fun or the enjoyment of being with friends. She worries too much about whether the food will be hot, the drinks will be cold, the guests will be on time. Her mind is filled with concerns:

Is the house clean enough, or will people think I'm a poor housekeeper? Will I run out of something? When the guests arrive, she becomes even more worried and anxious as she watches them all to make sure they are having a good time. After they leave, she is continually troubled by the thought that they might not have experienced the perfect evening. Since she is unable to relax before, during, or after the event, she misses out on what should be a pleasurable social activity.

LONELINESS AND DEPRESSION

The impossible quest for the perfect often affects relationships in a negative way. Loneliness and depression are the dual plagues of perfectionists, often because of their fear of rejection over being judged as imperfect. They believe that they must be perfect to be accepted, so they have a basic fear of expressing and experiencing feelings of closeness and affection. If others get too close, they will see the imperfections. This belief keeps perfectionists isolated and unable to accept warmth and help from others.

The English novel *Clarissa*, written by Samuel Richardson in the mid-1700s, gives us an extensive look at how perfectionism feeds into interpersonal conflicts, especially within families. The heroine suffers in her relationships, both within and beyond her family. But nowhere is the conflict seen more clearly than within the family. Even though the family members are portrayed as very unpleasant people, the reader sees there is another side to the conflict.

> **Sister Bella gets up late and comes downstairs untidy, to be greeted by the silent reproaches of an impeccably dressed Clarissa, who always rises at dawn. Brother James is wasting his university education, and Clarissa does not scruple to lecture him about it. The passive Mrs. Harlowe becomes sickly; Clarissa takes over her mother's neglected duties and performs them, of course, to perfection. Her perfectionistic solution, designed to protect her from hostility, succeeds only in generating more.[7]**

It's hard to have sympathy for her because in the novel it is much easier to see how she brings out the hostility of those around her.

The tragedy is that Clarissa is all too human. The struggles of perfectionists are much like her struggles, as she seemingly will do anything to maintain the image of her ideal self. In the end, she literally dies for that purpose—dies a martyr, purified and full of faith. Instead of accepting her real self, she is destroyed by her ideal self. Instead of releasing her creativity, she becomes a prisoner of her perfectionism.

Clarissa learned her perfectionism in her home. It is where most perfectionists learn theirs. It is also the place where they let it loose. And like Clarissa, their perfectionistic tendencies make it difficult, if not impossible, for them to relate to those they love. In their families and with their friends they become spoilers. They demand too much and offer too little.

Living with a perfectionist is not easy. All too often, a perfectionist thinks that happiness comes from having a perfect spouse, a perfect environment, perfect friends, perfect circumstances. When a perfectionist first meets someone, that person is idealized and perceived as being perfect. Things couldn't be better. But as the relationship progresses and the individuals get to know each other better or after they get married, the fantasy collapses. The other person is seen realistically, with faults and foibles. No longer a prince or a princess, the individual becomes a project. It's time to perfect the now imperfect spouse. It takes a strong spouse living with a perfectionist to be able to do what one perfectionist described: "Without question, my wife has been the most influential in 'calling my bluff' when my perfectionism gets out of hand. She has learned how to lovingly guide me back to reality." Another one said that her friends were strong enough to keep after her and, as she described it, continue "loving and accepting me, warts and all!"

Those living with a perfectionist find that it is often difficult to get to know that person. Perfectionists will work just as hard at keeping others from knowing them as they will at changing others; they will often retreat, raising their walls and pulling in the drawbridge. They are afraid of being found wanting in some way. One woman said that it took her years to realize that "a man is not going to marry me because I am not perfect." She went on to add, "Sometimes I'm okay about this, but most times I get very depressed about it."

This woman often finds fault with herself when friendships don't work. She's not young enough, not thin enough, or not sexy enough. In other words, if she were perfect, her friendships would work out. What she fails to see is that she is missing out on life; her excuses keep her at arm's length from others. When she has found a man who expresses interest in her, she is quick to find fault with him and send him on his way. The last long-term friendship she had was with a man who was just as perfectionistic as she is. The friendship survived several years of each one trying to remake the other into what each thought the perfect person should be like. Of course, this was done primarily from the safety of each person hiding behind the walls they had erected to keep from getting too close.

Getting close is the experience perfectionists desire most, but it is also the most frightening experience they can imagine. It's not that their outrageous demands about the quality of other persons are really true. They are simply a camouflage to hide the real feelings of helplessness, insecurity, and the need to relate to a superhuman to make up for the real or imagined deficiencies within. They miss out on the real thing—"the needing and being needed, the ups and downs, lovely moments, tedious afternoons, fights, gentleness, affection, humor. They miss out on *life*. They dream and the years go by."[8]

Most of the perfectionists we talked with said that the common emotional experience for them was depression. They become depressed when they can't do something perfectly:

- "I feel crushed. It takes a lot of mental rationalizing to pick up and go on."

- "I'll really be down in the dumps about it."

- "Logically I explain; emotionally I condemn myself."

- "I *relive* it for days and weeks and months and sometimes years."

- "I feel like the scum of the earth. I berate myself."

- "I try not to become depressed."

I often see these people for counseling because their emotional pain finally leads them to seek help. What quickly becomes the issue is the pattern of chronic difficulties in intimate relations with others. They will unconsciously discourage others and alienate them while consciously seeking to relate in a friendly manner.

Because they must remain somewhat distant from others to keep from being seen as less than perfect, perfectionists cannot afford to express opinions and feelings. They tend to think and say and do what they believe *others* want them to think and say and do. This lack of self-disclosure makes it very difficult for others to get close to them.

Because perfectionists hold on to the ideal relationship in their minds, they can easily end up single, lonely, isolated, and depressed. David Burns has noted "a high incidence of perfectionistic attitudes in people suffering from depressive illness. . . . [They] are likely to respond to the perception of failure or inadequacy with a precipitous loss of self-esteem that can trigger episodes of severe depression and anxiety."[9] Perfectionism is a vicious cycle that, instead of protecting people, leads them into the lonely, isolated trap they want to avoid. It can be a prison.

The Addiction to Perfection

*I can't look back on anything I have done
and feel proud and satisfied.*

We've looked at how the perfectionist struggles with obsessive-compulsive behavior patterns and with problems in relationships that lead to loneliness and depression. In addition, the perfectionist is also often at risk of impaired physical health.

TYPE A BEHAVIOR

During the 1960s, two cardiologists, Meyer Friedman and Ray Rosenman, began to study what they called *coronary-prone behavior patterns*. When they published the results of their studies in 1974, they called the coronary-prone pattern *Type A behavior*. The person exhibiting this type of behavior has been described as aggressive and extremely competitive, has a need to be in control and a desire for power, is impatient, and shows a high degree of perfectionism.

The problems associated with the physical health of these people are complicated by the fact that these traits are highly valued in today's society. With society's emphasis on fast-paced progress, high technology, and urbanization, people who show Type A behavior—who are aggressive, competitive, and perfectionistic—in the work force are rewarded. But according to Friedman and Rosenman, they are also at high risk for fatal heart attacks.

According to Mark Lipton, assistant professor at the Graduate School of Management in the New School for Social Research, New York, more recent studies show that Type A behavior is really counterproductive in much the same way that perfectionism is counterproductive. Lipton found that companies actually reward Type A behavior, equating it with success, even though it may not be healthy for either the individual or the organization. He went so far as to say that Type A behavior is "actually inconsistent with effective management."[1]

Type A behavior is characterized by a need to operate at full speed, which means that an individual feels a need to do more than one thing at a time. There is also an urgency to everything, causing the setting of unrealistic goals. For perfectionists, these unrealistic goals can be a hedge against future criticism.

Also like perfectionists in general, Type A people play to win. As a result, they are very critical of their own performance and don't hesitate to criticize someone else's performance. Although not all perfectionists are Type A people, Type A people have trouble with delegating responsibility. They feel that the only way to get the job done right is to do it themselves. Like perfectionists, Type A people have taken the desire to achieve and turned it into a compulsive drive that leaves little room for satisfaction.

The Type A behavior pattern in adults has received a lot of attention, but the roots of that pattern in children are just beginning to be studied. According to Carl Thoresen, professor of education and psychology at Stanford University, "children's responses to stress may provide important clues for understanding the origins of harmful behavior patterns in adults."[2]

Type A behavior is an attempt to control what is perceived as a demanding, challenging, and often hostile environment. As we have seen in looking at the roots of perfectionism, the budding perfectionist also sees the environment as potentially hostile and in need of being controlled. These developing tendencies within children appear to have physical consequences. Atherosclerosis is a gradual degenerating process in adults characterized by a clogging of the arteries. However, autopsies of young people often show evidence of this disease, indicating that the price for perfectionism and Type A behavior starts being paid in childhood.

Type A children tend to experience more anger than other children, but they are also more likely to keep that anger inside. These children also experience more anxiety and, as a group, have lower self-esteem. Thoreson found that these children push themselves harder but do not perform any better in tasks or do any better in school than other children. In addition, Type A children show a greater fear of sucess than non-Type A children.

The characteristics of Type A behavior include perfectionism, but in describing the symptoms in either children or adults, one could just as easily be describing the symptoms of perfectionistic behavior. Their successes, like those of perfectionists, are empty and meaningless. Jonathan Sachs, the founder of Lotus Software, lost his family creating a product for which he has no feeling. He has made more than $13 million; yet, he's still looking for a cause to give his life meaning. What Type A people and perfectionists fail to recognize is that point, which is different for each person, where "the joy of doing a task well gives way to the fear of not doing it perfectly."[3]

SUBSTANCE ABUSE

It's easier to see perfectionistic behaviors in Type A people than it is in alcoholics or substance abusers. Perhaps the main reason for this is that we tend to judge these people and their behavior by how they act when they are drunk or under the influence of a drug. But to understand alcoholics better, we must look more closely at their sober behavior and attitudes.

One study reported:

Rather than being uncontrolled, reckless, and unashamed, sober alcoholics are generally

cautious, careful, often overcontrolled and inhibited. They are always guilt ridden. In contrast to the stereotyped alcoholic who is seen as irresponsible, negligent, disorderly, and indifferent, the sober alcoholic is usually highly responsible, conscientious, orderly, cautious, and often perfectionist, placing inordinately high performance demands upon himself.[4]

The sober alcoholic is a hard worker and a driven perfectionist who is unable to relax and let go. Part of this behavior is in response to the guilt felt as a result of the drinking, but a large part of it is due to the underlying perfectionism of nearly every substance abuser.

The codependent, or non-drinking friend or family member, of the substance abuser is usually just as perfectionistic. Everything in the environment must be in perfect order. If the codependent is the wife, the house must be perfect; everything must be in its place. One wife said, "I realized I was a perfectionist when I found myself lying on my back on the kitchen floor with my head as far under the radiator as possible, trying to flick or blow off every last vestige of dust."[5] The drive for perfection by the family members of the alcoholic is amplified by the fear that anything out of the ordinary or out of place could set the alcoholic off on a drinking binge or cause the drug addict to use.

The recognition of this drivenness is noted in the opening of the prayer used by recovering alcoholics and their codependents, "God grant me the serenity to accept the things I cannot change." Some researchers believe that part of the reason the alcoholic drinks is to find serenity in a world where nothing is good enough.

A major part of the recovery of the alcoholic or drug addict is to become less of a perfectionist. But the same thing that keeps the perfectionist from reaching out for help and keeps the substance abuser stuck is an exaggerated sense of self-reliance. One alcoholic said, "I've always tried to do everything on my own. I guess the fact that I can't control my drinking means I'm not as great as I like to think I am. And if I'm not great, I feel I'm weak, like a wheel with a spoke missing."[6]

Brian L., a recovering alcoholic, wrote a booklet on perfectionism in which he said,

> **As perfectionistic people, we simply expect too much of ourselves and others. Our attitudes keep us from using recovery methods, including the Twelve Steps of Alcoholics Anonymous, which could lead us to a contented sobriety. People with perfectionistic values are true children of our individualistic society. They feel they must solve their problem of being chemically dependent by fighting it and trying to defeat it. But this problem will not be resolved through will-power or attempts to control ourselves or other people.[7]**

The ability to accept oneself, with imperfection, is crucial to recovery.

He went on to note that perfectionists and substance abusers suffer from low self-esteem, practice self-criticism, and have a tremendous fear of failure. "The habit of procrastination is another form of our fear of failure," he added. "If we think we must perform our tasks perfectly, all too often we put off even trying."[8] These behaviors are not only self-defeating; they are part of a self-destructive cycle.

Karl Menninger recognized the self-destructive part of alcoholism, referring to it as a form of chronic suicide. He said,

Alcohol addiction . . . can be considered a form of self-destruction used to avert a greater self-destruction deriving from elements of aggressiveness . . . , and the feeling of a need for punishment from a sense of guilt related to aggressiveness. Its further quality is that in a practical sense self-destruction is accomplished by means of the very device used by the sufferer to relieve his pain and avert his fear of destruction.[9]

One alcoholic observed that he drank because of the continuing failure to maintain himself in some imaginary position of perfection. Later in his recovery he was able to see the self-destructive aspect of his behavior as a form of self-punishment for failing to be God.

Other studies of drug addicts show a similar perfectionistic pattern as in alcoholics. One study found that users of LSD, heroin, and alcohol share similar family backgrounds and often start using the chemical as a means to reduce stress in their lives. This use of a drug to lessen stress is common to our culture. Most people use prescription drugs for that purpose, but some choose to use illegal drugs or alcohol to accomplish the same thing. This use of a chemical to reduce stress may help to explain why adolescence and other stressful transition periods are often associated with the most severe drug and alcohol problems.

PHYSICAL ILLNESS

We noted in the last chapter that one of the emotional consequences of perfectionism is depression. At the root of this depression is a rage that grows out of the impossibility of the perfectionistic lifestyle. This rage is turned inward on the self and can manifest itself in the form of depression, or it can shift its focus and become the trigger for a number of physical illnesses.

We've looked at how the perfectionism of Type A people makes them highly at risk for heart attacks. Other illnesses to which perfectionists are prone include arthritis, ulcerative colitis, atypical facial pain, and anorexia.

An interesting study was made of a number of people suffering from ulcerative colitis. The researchers were looking for common factors that might explain the development of the illness. All of the patients described themselves as nervous, and almost all said they were overscrupulously perfectionistic.[10]

Another study focused on atypical facial pain. This

type of pain is one of the most agonizing forms that can
be experienced, partly because of the makeup of nerves
in the face and partly because the face is so much a part
of an individual's self-awareness. Atypical facial pain
does not follow typical nerve distribution areas. Instead, it tends to be deep, diffuse, and poorly localized,
lasting anywhere from hours to days. Researchers in-
vestigating the personality factors of patients suffering
from this illness found that perfectionism was the most
common trait shared by both men and women.[11]

Several years ago, I worked with a woman who had
suffered almost every day over a ten-year period from
atypical facial pain. Her neurologist had suggested that
she see me because of the depression she was experiencing due to her unresolved pain. Over the course of
her therapy, it became increasingly clear to her that she
had spent her adult life trying to be someone she
wasn't. Both the nature of her work and the expectations of her husband demanded this of her. She was a
perfectionist, so she tried to be what she was expected
to be, and she had to do it perfectly! When she worked
through the inner rage she felt at not being allowed to
be herself and reduced her perfectionistic behavior so
that she could give herself permission to be her real
self, the pain became almost nonexistent. Any experience of pain in her face after that was minimal and no
longer interfered with her life.

I talked recently with a perfectionist who battles
both depression and arthritis. He sets extremely high
standards for himself in his work as well as with his

family. His role in his extended family is to be the counselor for everyone as well as the primary channel of communication for family members who are upset with other family members. He has recently found that he is the counselor at work, too, listening to fellow employees' problems frequently. Of course his perfectionism does not allow him to say no to anyone, nor does it allow him to express any anger or frustration over his "duties" within the family. When his pent-up anger switched from being directed toward his emotions as depression, he started to develop the pain and symptoms of rheumatoid arthritis in his arms and legs. When the pressures build, so does the pain. When the pressures let up, so does the pain. His medical doctor told him that unless he learned how to stop being a perfectionist, the pain and the arthritis would become more permanent.

Impotence has been related directly to perfectionistic thinking. Often men who are impotent have the belief that they must always perform perfectly in intercourse. When a man experiences impotence, he attaches it to a feeling of personal inadequacy and failure. A study designed to examine the emotional causes of impotence found that perfectionism was one of the three consistent factors.[12]

ANOREXIA NERVOSA AND OTHER EATING DISORDERS

Anorexia nervosa is another form of self-destruction that leads to lifelong problems or even to death. Today's plague of eating disorders is not new. Anorexia was described in various ways in the sixteenth and seventeenth centuries, but it is a rapidly growing illness in our culture. Approximately 90 to 95 percent of anorexics are women, with male cases being reported with increasing frequency. The typical anorexic looks like a walking skeleton—legs sticking out like broomsticks, every rib showing, and shoulder blades looking like little wings. *Anorexia* is the deliberate and severe loss of weight by the restriction of food intake or by a compulsive exercise program that burns more calories than are consumed. *Bulimia* is the attempt to control weight by purging, either by vomiting or by overusing laxatives.

There is no clear, consistent picture of the emotional makeup of the person with an eating disorder. Some common characteristics have been noted, which include a pattern of low self-esteem—in spite of high achievements—and perfectionism.[13] The typical person with anorexia is highly self-critical and experiences herself as inadequate in much the same way as many other perfectionists. However, her perfectionism has become focused on weight as a way to evaluate herself. It is easy to see how a young female suffering from feelings of inadequacy might decide that her weight would be a good way to evaluate herself. After all, everything in our culture says that thin is good. Therefore, to feel good about herself, she becomes thin.

What the anorexic experiences has been described as "a cycle of inflationary self-evaluations" in which "replication of past excellence becomes routinely expected and future endeavors must always set new highs."[14] The anorexic says, "If only I weighed a little bit less, I would feel better about myself." But when she loses that weight, she is not satisfied for very long; she must lose more weight to satisfy herself, and on and on it goes. Soon, it is not the loss of the weight that is important, it is the *losing* of the weight. This cycle was mentioned earlier about other forms of perfectionism; people lose sight of the goal of their behavior and focus instead on the perfect doing of the behavior. Achievement is secondary to perfection. Weight loss is secondary to losing weight. Eventually, nothing else matters.

The overeater can be a perfectionist in much the same way as the alcoholic or the anorexic. Instead of an addiction to alcohol or to losing weight, the overeater is addicted to food. One woman, who weighed over three hundred pounds, found in therapy that she had a deep longing for the perfect. Her perfectionism was so strong that she had created an idealized world within her imagination. Over the years, she had grown to hate the real world, including her obese body. She said that the pain of living forced her to create a new life in an unreal world where everything was ideal. In her fantasy world, she was thin and lovely. There were no problems; everything was perfect.

For this woman, dieting was facing the real world, and with that, she came face-to-face with her own imperfection. When the anxiety of the real world would overwhelm her, she would eat and then retreat back into the fantasy world of her imagination. For her, as for any perfectionist, her dream of perfection was the root of her defeat and self-destruction.

The pursuit of perfection is an obsession, whether it is an obsession with alcohol, drugs, food, weight, job, or emotional peace and harmony. The obsession determines where the focus of one's energy will be, and that becomes the addiction. To be addicted to anything is to choose the object of addiction over life—over reality. The result of striving for perfection is giving up on living.

Help! I Live with a Perfectionist

To talk about the need for perfection in man is to talk
about the need for another species. The essence of man
is imperfection. Imperfection and blazing contra-
dictions—between mixed good and evil, altruism
and selfishness, co-operativeness and
combativeness, optimism and fatalism,
affirmation and negation.
—Norman Cousins

*P*erfectionism is not a very rewarding lifestyle, to say the least. If we live with perfectionists, we see and experience their frustration. If we are the perfectionists, we know the struggle firsthand. So why don't people just quit being so perfectionistic? They read articles and books that tell them what to do. They talk to friends, and they talk to themselves, determined to change—only to wake up the next day just as perfectionistic as before. So help! What's a perfectionist to do?

The basic area of need appears to be the redefining, and even the rediscovery, of the real self. As we saw in chapter 4, most of perfectionism grows out of the development of the ideal self as a means to avoid anxiety, hurt, and disappointment in the early stages of growth.

If people are going to free themselves, or those they love, from the prison of perfectionism, they need to dig out the roots of perfectionism as well as remove the behaviors.

These roots are difficult for individuals to see in themselves because, in most circumstances, they provide an adequate coping style for dealing with life. People notice the inadequacy of perfectionism as a standard when it comes into conflict with another important value. For example, a divorced woman who is now a single parent feels that she needs to be the ideal mother, giving her time and energy to her children. But she must also be the ideal employee at work where she holds an important middle management position. Because she is in management, she must put in the hours needed to do her job, but at the same time, she must be available to her children. On top of that, when does she have time for her own social life? In this situation, she might try to untie the Gordian knot by quickly finding a new spouse, but even if that were possible, she would only be adding a third role—that of new wife—to the other two demanding her perfection. Her perfectionism, which in its early stages of development was designed to alleviate feelings of hurt and anxiety, only creates additional anxiety and added potential for hurt.

When someone is caught in this trap, it is easy to externalize struggles: "If only I had a spouse!" "If only I didn't have kids!" "If only I had more money!" "If only I'd get a promotion or the raise I've been promised!" Or the perfectionist may project personal standards and demands onto other people: "If only my kids were less trouble!" "If only I had more competent people working for me!" "If only I had a better management team, they would recognize how good I am!" "Why did I have to marry that jerk? Life would be better without having to deal with all these added problems!" If it weren't for all the external forces pressing in, everything would be perfect!

The other attempt to resolve these kinds of conflicts is to simply try harder and deny the existence of any feelings of conflict. Trying harder is a subtle trap. It takes most people a long time to learn that trying harder only produces more of the same thing trying to be avoided. The single parent of our example can deny any feelings of conflict between her role as mother and her role as middle manager. She can simply grit her teeth and run faster—work those hours, stay up late sewing the kids' costumes for the Christmas pageant or cooking special birthday cakes, spend the weekend doing things with the kids out of guilt over the time not spent with them during the week. And always with a *strained* smile on her face. In truth, the only thing she does allow herself to feel is strain. The harder she tries, the less effective she is at her job of mother and her job as manager. She desperately needs to redefine her understanding of herself so that her real self can begin to grow.

REDEFINING SELF IN TERMS
OF RELATIONSHIPS

To get at the roots of perfectionism, we must go back to the beginnings of our development. For all of us, the consistent presence or absence of a primary mothering person during the early stages of life provides the major factor in tying together whatever we are today.

It is through her that body, impulse, feeling, action, and eventually thought become organized as part of the self and integrated not only with each other but also with external reality of which she is a representative. She is a bridge between the child's inner world of experience and the outer world of reality.[1]

The mothering person's role in the development of the self is critical. When early development goes well, the outcome is the achievement of a healthy real self.

Problems related to the real self, including perfectionism, result from failures of this process. All of us have experienced failures in this process because no one can handle the mothering process perfectly. The acceptance of the reality of the process helps each of us accept the reality of the real self.

But I have found that people will go to any lengths to avoid looking at the reality of their personal mothering process. Horney said that the most common way they do this is to alienate the real self, even to the point of sending it into exile.[2] They suppress one aspect of reality and focus on another—once again an example of all-or-nothing thinking. All of this is done in the name of preserving the self. But what is being preserved is the ideal self.

One successful businessman I talked with equated much of his success with his perfectionism. When we started to look at his family history, it was easy for him to describe the deficits he experienced in his relationship with both his mother and his father. But before we could begin to look at how he felt about any of those experiences, he quickly pointed out that his mom had her own problems and that she did the best she could.

I quickly agreed with him, but I wanted to get back to how he felt about it. He added, "I don't think about it. I try to make the time we are together as pleasant as possible." His reason for coming to see me was to look at why he had so much trouble building relationships. The process of our talking together focused more and more on how he practiced all-or-nothing thinking in regard to his family relationships, and that same pattern seemed to work in his current relationships. The more interested he became in the truth about himself and his relationships within his family of origin, the more he started to assume responsibility for his part of his relational problems.

The most difficult parts of our discussions were focused on his right to be angry about those deficits in his childhood experiences. It was true that his mom did the best she could, but that did not take away his right to be angry about what he missed.

Probably one of the clearest indicators that the real self is back in charge is "the establishment of a relationship of equality with one's parents."[3] This equality is not established once and for all, but requires a continuing process of believing in and reaffirming that equality. Often, this process doesn't involve the real parents in any direct way. It is actually focused on the internalized parents, that internal idealized picture of what we wish our parents were like.

I must state emphatically that this is *not* a blaming process, for we already noted that one way to keep the real self in exile is to place all the blame for one's problems on others. The purpose is not to blame the mothering person, but to arrive at a point of equality with that person in one's own mind.

REDEFINING SELF IN TERMS OF EMOTIONS

I touched on this subject when I spoke of the right to be angry with the mothering person in one's life for the deficits in what one wishes had been provided. To do this, a person must begin to feel emotions. The denial of feelings is one of the chief ways to keep the real self in exile, out of one's personal awareness and out of everyone else's awareness. If someone can eliminate the real self and project inner experiences on other people by placing the blame on them, the individual can work on perfection and the development of the ideal self. But emotions are a source of danger in that process, for they are intimately connected with the real self.

Perfectionism, with its gallant attempt at conscious self-control, must always keep a check on impulses and any outbursts of anger or enthusiasm. It acts like a burglar alarm or a fire alarm. Whenever unwanted feelings (which are most of them) start to arise, the alarm goes off, usually signaling the fear that the individual might appear less than ideal.

Usually, all feelings are kept under tight control, even the positive ones of joy and affection. Jealousy and resentment are able to grow in such a sterile environment, but not much else. The body shows it through the way the individual breathes and walks; sometimes the individual shows it through a sense of dignity, poise, or stoicism. Whatever the cost, feelings must be controlled!

Another way this is evident is in the choice to place ultimate value in the mind. Sometimes this supremacy of the mind allows a person to express feelings to a degree, but they must always be examined and analyzed—and especially controlled—by the mind. "Thus, factually, another dualism is created. It is no longer mind *and* body but mind *versus* body; no longer mind *and* self but mind *versus* self."[4] Again, it is the all-or-nothing, either-or type of perfectionistic thinking. A person becomes a spectator of life when the mind is supreme.

Alcoholics, as perfectionistic people, have learned how to deal with this issue of control. The key is recovery from chemical dependency and from perfectionism. Although recovery is built upon the Twelve Steps of Alcoholics Anonymous, the first three steps are particularly important to perfectionists.

Step One asks people to admit that they are limited human beings and that chemical use and character defects, such as perfectionism, have made their lives unmanageable. This admission of powerlessness is neither natural nor easy. But if they are to begin to redefine the self in the area of emotions, they must begin with an admission of humility and powerlessness. Members of Alcoholics Anonymous learn that "admissions of personal powerlessness finally turn out to be firm bedrock upon which happy and purposeful lives may be built."[5] When persons ask why they must do this, the answer is that if they want to change their attitudes and experience the real self and their emotions, they must "hit bottom" first. They must give up the pride of the ideal self.

Step Two describes the realization that individuals cannot handle their chemical dependency or their perfectionism by themselves. Instead, they must look to God for help. Only a power greater than themselves can restore them. Just as few alcoholics have any idea how irrational they are, few perfectionists can bear to look at the irrationality of their perfectionism. Only when they stop attempting to be God and place their faith in him can they continue the process of recovery.

Step Three is the opening of a door that may still

seem to be closed. But this step is the key to the opening of the door. People are required to surrender their will and control to God, willing to believe that they have limitations and imperfections, and willing to act as if that is really true. This is an active step. It requires individuals to *make a decision* to turn their will over to God. In many ways, this step is not only the beginning of change, but is a giant step in the process of change itself. Recovering alcoholics admit that "our whole trouble has been the misuse of willpower. We had tried to bombard our problems with it instead of attempting to bring it into agreement with God's intention for us."[6] Perfectionists have the same problem.

Taking these three steps in the area of the emotions breathes new life into the real self. They form the basis for the Serenity Prayer, which says, "God grant me the serenity to accept the things I cannot change, courage to change the things I can, and the wisdom to know the difference. Thy will, not mine, be done."

Sometimes this process is blocked by an inability to feel anything. Horney quoted a patient as saying,

I saw that I was quite simply unable to *want* anything, not even death! And certainly not "life." Until now I had thought my trouble was just that I was unable to *do* things; unable to give up my dream, unable to gather up own things, unable to accept or control my irritability, unable to make myself more human, whether by sheer will power, patience, or grief.

> Now for the first time I saw it—I was liter-
> ally unable to *feel* anything. (Yes, for all my
> famous supersensitivity!) How well I knew
> pain—every pore of me clogged with inward
> rage, self-pity, self-contempt, and despair for
> the last six years and over and over again and
> again! Yet I saw it now—all was negative, reac-
> tive, compulsive, *all imposed from without;* in-
> side there was absolutely nothing of mine.[7]

A person's feelings don't have to be negative to be
make-believe—they can just as readily be saintly, generous, and *perfectly* lovely. The solution is to find some
way to begin to listen to one's inner wisdom—to listen
to the feelings of the real self. To do this, an individual
may want to get into a Twelve Step program in AA or
in Alanon. The same thing may be accomplished by becoming accountable to someone else, the same way a
person in recovery becomes accountable to a sponsor.

Writing is a helpful part of this process—for example, taking the time to listen to yourself and writing
down what is in your mind *and* heart. Taking a day off
to sit at the beach or in the forest and do nothing but
listen to yourself can turn the volume up so a person
can actually begin to hear what the real self is all about.
Recovering alcoholics do this with Step Four when they
take a "searching and fearless moral inventory" of
themselves.

Working with a therapist can also help to bring
someone in touch with the emotions associated with the

real self, the feelings locked away deep inside. Sometimes a therapist or a sponsor can make the process less frightening. Sometimes these helpers can keep someone going who is beginning to get bogged down. Redefining the self in terms of the emotions usually requires some kind of guide, for the journey is quite difficult, especially at the beginning.

REDEFINING SELF IN TERMS
OF BALANCE

Parts of the process of redefining the self in terms of balance have been started as individuals work on the other two areas of redefining the self. What this means is that perfectionists begin to weave back together the fragmented parts of the self that have developed because of their tendency to compartmentalize life. As we discussed earlier, because they try harder, they divide up aspects of themselves, splitting them off to keep from dealing with them.

Carl Jung, the Swiss psychiatrist, saw this compartmentalizing in terms of the masculine and feminine parts of the self in each person. He identified perfection with the masculine because it is part of the basic spiritual search of humankind. What he called the *anthropos archetype* is at the root of our spirituality. That's why so many psychotic types of behavior take on a religious theme; the person who has lost total touch with reality starts out being Napoleon and ends up believing he is Jesus Christ.

The problem with our age is that we have become so scientific that we are uncomfortable with our spiritual roots. So people externalize this search and separate consciously from God so that it becomes the "drive for glory" or perfectionism. Jung said that perfection is a masculine desire, "while woman inclines by nature to completeness."⁸ This is part of the reason why perfectionism seems to be a greater problem with women than with men. Any time a woman strives for perfection, she is neglecting the role of completeness. The masculine role of perfection and the feminine role of completeness are complementary, and neither one is complete or perfect without the other. Jung added that, "just as completeness is always imperfect, so perfection is always incomplete, and therefore represents a final state which is hopelessly sterile."⁹ If either one is sought by itself—perfection or completeness—the person can only end up in a blind alley.

Because perfectionists cannot internalize the spiritual search, because the real self is in exile, they cannot experience wholeness. As Jung was prone to do, he traced this struggle through history, seeing the religious wars as examples of this struggle on a larger scale. Certainly, most religious wars have been fought for the purpose of purifying the faith to arrive at a more perfect church and a more perfect society. But in the case of religious wars, as well as in perfectionists' resistance to the spiritual reality of faith, this drive can be controlling and can lead to a perfection that is one-sided or compartmentalized, not to wholeness.

Jung observed that

the more the feminine ideal is bent in the direction of the masculine, the more the woman loses her power to compensate the masculine striving for perfection, and a typically masculine ideal state arises. . . . No path leads beyond perfection into the future—there is only a turning back, a collapse of the ideal, which could easily have been avoided by paying attention to the feminine ideal of completeness.[10]

He was talking about keeping a healthy balance within the self that seeks wholeness.

Perfectionists have within them what they need to break the hold that perfectionism has upon them. They must reintegrate the various aspects of their all-or-nothing thinking. They need to realize that the perfect does not exist; therefore, no one is perfectly good or perfectly bad. Everyone is a balance of both.

I had an experience that illustrates this. For years, I have had a negative view of uniformed police officers driving police cars. I have friends who are police officers, but as long as they are not in uniform or driving a police car, I have no problem. I have compartmentalized this part of my experience, perhaps because of what I consider unfair treatment when I was first starting to drive. Two police officers stopped me and took me to the police station. There they decided what my fine was and divided the cash before I left. Jan has stated that I have a problem with authority, but I am quick to point out that it is only a problem with uniformed police officers in police cars.

My anger boils when I see police officers stopping people. (The same thing happens when they stop *me*, but I have been careful to control my reactions.) I get especially angry when I see them stopping young people. But I get even angrier about people who drink and drive.

One evening as I pulled out of the driveway of my office building, I saw that the other lane was blocked by a police car. Apparently, the uniformed officer had stopped a car with two young men in it. My first reaction was to be angry with the policeman until I noticed that on the roof of the car were four open cans of beer. Immediately, my anger was redirected toward the young men. I had two competing values at war within myself, and I didn't know where to place my anger. All the way home that evening, I struggled with my emotions, not knowing what I really felt. I thought about what I had experienced when I was sixteen and just beginning to drive. I thought about the number of deaths caused by drinking and driving. I talked with Jan about it when I got home.

Eventually, I decided that not all young people who are stopped by the police are getting unfair treatment. Sometimes they deserve to be stopped. I decided that not every police officer is unfair to teens. But sometimes unfair treatment does occur; sometimes teens get stopped just because they are teens. After all, police officers aren't perfect—they sometimes make mistakes, but most of the time they don't.

That all sounds very simple and clear as I write it now. But that night driving home, it wasn't simple or clear. I was getting rid of a "compartment" in my thinking that helped to keep part of my real self in exile. And since then, I've noticed that I don't get upset when I see a police officer stopping someone—as long as it isn't me. To get free of the anxiety I felt as a result of that inner conflict, I had to find a balance that allowed people to be human.

Redefining the self really means finding the real self again and encouraging it to grow stronger. I had to do that in the area of authority in my life. The single mom we talked about at the beginning of the chapter needs to find a balance within herself that allows her to be human, with shortcomings and limitations. Following these five important steps will help her or any perfectionist dig out the roots of perfectionism so that the real self can grow. I have directly addressed the perfectionist in the next section and have included some exercises to be completed there, but the individual living with a perfectionist can benefit, too, by following through each step and gaining an understanding of the process involved in allowing the real self to grow.

STEP ONE: MAKE CHANGE YOUR PRIORITY

Decide that, no matter what is required, you will begin to make changes in your life regarding your perfectionism. In the same way that you have committed yourself to being perfect, make a commitment to yourself to change those patterns. It is important to think of the word *change* because some of you may think that change is to become more perfect at being perfect. What you are doing here is beginning the process that will make changes in your life that involve *giving up* being or doing the perfect.

You've started the process by reading this book. But it's only the beginning. You are making a commitment to a *process* that will involve many changes. This is the first step—to make change your priority.

Decide now that you will make change a priority, and write your commitment here:

I am committing myself to

STEP TWO: COURAGEOUSLY CHOOSE TO
BE LESS THAN PERFECT

The first step is a decision. The second step involves action. Define areas of your life where you have been perfectionistic and list them on the next page.

Now comes the risky part. Take one of these areas of perfectionism and describe to yourself how you would act or what you would do if you could be satisfied with a less-than-perfect result. How would you begin? What would be a "good enough" job that would keep everyone happy, including you?

One woman described how she would spend hours at work giving 100 percent in preparing reports. When she started working on her perfectionism, she evaluated what her co-workers did and found that they gave about 80 percent to the task and spent about 20 percent of their effort on building relationships with other co-workers. What really opened her eyes was the realization that the extra effort she put into her reports made absolutely no difference in the eyes of her boss. She decided that she would courageously choose to be less than perfect from that point on.

Write down how you will be different in one area of your perfectionism:

STEP THREE: KEEP A JOURNAL
OF YOUR EMOTIONS

Since allowing the real self to grow requires you to look again at your emotions, you will need to do something concrete about what your inner wisdom is saying to you. Writing is a very effective way to understand your emotions better.

What do you write? Anything. Everything. There are no hard and fast rules, at least to get started. Begin by looking at what you feel good about and what makes you frustrated or upset. Make lists. Write down key words. Write a story. Write down everything that enters your mind. Examine what is going on in your life now. Write about the hurts of the past—how did you feel then? Look at some of your fears of the future. Where are you struggling now?

If you find this helpful, you may choose to attend a workshop on journal writing. The interesting thing about writing is that it brings feelings into the real world in a comfortable, controlled way. A lot of times, people fear that if they begin to look at feelings, they will quickly be overwhelmed by the feelings and lose control completely. Not if you write. The process of writing controls the flow of emotion. Getting the feelings out into the real world in concrete form on paper releases those feelings and allows more to come.

Sometimes writing an angry letter to an important person who let you down in your past can be healing, bringing closure to that part of your past. Of course, the letter is never given to that person, so it is effective even if the person has died. As people in the recovery process of Alcoholics Anonymous have found, spending time talking with a trusted person about what you have written can help finish the task. All you need is a listener—someone who cares for you and has your trust. Write down who that person might be for you:

STEP FOUR: BE SELFISH

I use the word *selfish* on purpose so that I can catch your attention and then explain more fully what I mean. I often say this to people in therapy and then wait for their reaction. Often it is just like yours—negative.

For most of us, the word *selfish* is understood in a negative way to mean "cruel, thoughtless, noncaring." For a lot of us, our spiritual background is repelled by that thought because it conveys the idea of putting self first. To help you understand the way I use the word, let's put all those negative connotations under the heading of *self-centered.* Everything we have previously attached to *selfish* is now attached to *self-centered.*

Selfish as I use it means that you consciously decide to take care of yourself first, instead of last. It means that you will begin to listen to that inner wisdom of the real self that knows what is good for you, what is right for you, what is healthy for you. It means that you are a person of worth and value and that if you are to be the best you can be, you must take care of yourself.

Let me illustrate the difference. A self-centered person can be a very self-giving person. This person may have the habit of writing out checks to anyone in need. If you need something, you will receive a check to meet that need. But this person may be so busy giving out checks that there is no time to look at the balance and make certain that there is money in the account. So a lot of worthless checks are written. This individual has become self-centered in order to preserve a very fragile and inadequate sense of self. That's why it is so hard for a self-centered person to receive anything. It is frightening to be the focus of attention.

The selfish person is also a self-giving person who has a checking account and will write you a check if you are in need. But sometimes you will be told no, for there is nothing in the account. Instead of helping you, the individual must take the time to go to the bank and make a deposit. Sometimes the selfish person may question your need; thus, you may discover some way to have your need met instead of relying on someone else. The selfish person cares enough about you to care about self. By taking responsibility for self, making certain to take care of self, the selfish person has something to give.

Being selfish means being less than perfect and being satisfied with giving the best you can give under the circumstances. Being selfish means you care enough about others to let them be responsible for themselves, so they can be free to take better care of themselves.

If you became selfish in this way, what are some things you would do for yourself? Write them here:

STEP FIVE: GET HELP

This could just as easily be the first step. Just make certain it is one of the steps. Because the roots of perfectionism go deep, you may have blind spots about where they are. To get help, give up the idea that you can do it yourself—that you can do it alone. Every perfectionist thinks it can be done better alone. But if you are going to break free, you are going to need help. Once you find someone to help, stick with your exploration of your perfectionism. It is easy to give up when the going gets tough, but that is the time you need help the most.

Getting help will take you beyond what we have examined in this book. Because the roots can run deep, the obstructive forces at work within you will be hard to break. But only when you have broken these forces will you find that the constructive forces of the real self have a chance to grow. Remember, you have made a commitment to change. That means no matter what the cost in time, money, or effort, you *will* change—you *will* get help.

If you are going to see a professional therapist, do not be intimidated by the person's degrees or training. You are hiring a consultant to help you, so find the best one to meet your needs. Is the consultant trained to help you with the roots of your perfectionism? Does the consultant ask questions about your family history that are similar to what we have talked about in this book? Take the time to meet several therapists, if necessary, until you find the one who is right for you.

We've looked at how perfectionists can get the roots of perfectionism out of their lives. Next we will look at constructive ways they can break the patterns of perfectionism and how those patterns affect behavior.

The Battleground Is the Mind

*I live with the "tyranny of the oughts," always
dissatisfied with the compromises I make to
balance family life, work, career advancement,
ministry, etc. In focusing on only one, I know I
am unbalanced and therefore failing. If I
balance the areas, I am not achieving.*

Once perfectionists have dug up the roots of their perfectionism, they are still left with the task of changing patterns of perfectionistic behaviors. How can these be changed? David Burns tells of a young law student named Jennifer who had been treated for depression but still struggled with the problem. She explained:

My therapist told me that my problem was perfectionism. She said I had impossible expectations, and I made excessive demands on myself. She traced the origins of my problem to my relationship with my mother. My mother is very compulsive and can find 16 things wrong with an incredibly clean room. The therapist suggested that if I would stop being so perfectionistic, I'd feel better, but she never told me how to go about doing that. I'd like to get over my perfectionism. But how do I proceed?[1]

Jennifer asked an important question. If I had stopped this book with the preceding chapter, many perfectionists would be left trying to answer the same question: "I understand now *why* I am perfectionistic. But what can I do about it?" It's one thing to be able to point out the root cause of perfectionism; it's quite another thing to be able to dig out the roots and change the pattern of growth. The problems associated with changing behaviors are all found in the way people think. The battleground is the mind.[2]

Most people operate on the assumption that events in life cause them to feel what they feel and do what they do. Research by Aaron Beck and David Burns has shown that this is not so. People feel what they feel and do what they do because of the way they think. Shakespeare's Hamlet seemed to understand this because he said, "There is nothing either good or bad, but thinking makes it so." Proverbs 23:7 says, "For as he thinks in his heart, so is he." Burns notes that "the perfectionists' dichotomous thinking and moralistic self-evaluations contribute to their psychological distress and cause them to adopt strategies for personal growth and self-management that are naive and self-defeating."[3] One of the most destructive thought patterns involves what Horney called *the tyranny of the "shoulds,"* discussed in chapter 1. She said "the more the shoulds become the sole motor force moving him, driving him, whipping him into action,"[4] the more stuck a person will be in perfectionism. If someone is going to break the behavior patterns of perfectionism, he or she will break the thought patterns that maintain the attitudes and behaviors.

In this chapter we will explore six practical ways to break the patterns of perfectionistic behavior once its roots have been cleared out.

1. RESET PERSONAL GOALS

Reexamining values and personal goals is the first step to modifying behavior. It's all right to have lists of things that need to be done, but it's important to remember that not everything must be done today or must be done perfectly.

Instead of setting goals as measures of achievement, a perfectionist might try to define a life purpose. "Why am I here on earth?" "How do I want to be remembered after I'm dead and gone?" These are some questions to be considered. Some goals may be set that are not related to career. For example, a goal could be, "I want to experience peace of mind." Then a way to reach that goal could be delineated.

Another way to reexamine goals is to imagine that one has only a year left to live. What effect would that have on the goals? The emphasis may shift from what can be achieved or accomplished to what can be experienced. These ideas can be incorporated into a statement of goals for life.

It helps to think of life goals as being stated in an abstract form. For example, my life goal is summed up in the statement, "I want to be an agent of healing in relationships." That is an abstract statement that allows for a variety of ways to be accomplished. For example, my wife, Jan, and I lead seminars that are designed to help people build better relationships. I write books, like this one, to help people build better relationships with themselves and others. And I work as a therapist with individuals and couples for the same purpose. Perhaps I will stop doing one of those and do something else, for my life goal is stated in such a way that I have a variety of ways to work toward it. Because it is a big abstraction, it is too big for me to ever fully accomplish, so I have flexibility in what I do.

Once life goals have been identified, realistic subgoals may be set. Sometimes perfectionists are driven by a need for closure to the point that they cannot rest until a task is finished. This tendency can be softened by setting subgoals that, when accomplished, give a sense of closure without the urgency of doing it all. And as the subgoals are accomplished, the individual will be moving steadily toward the accomplishment of larger goals without the anxiety of an unfinished or less-than-perfect effort.

An interesting exercise would be to set some subgoals that are actually mistakes. One of the most difficult things for perfectionists to believe is that mistakes are not total failures. In fact, people can often learn more from mistakes than from successes. Purposely setting out to make a mistake for the sake of learning can help in the development of more realistic goals. An example of this would be to set as a goal the accomplishment of something that has been avoided for fear of failure. Perhaps it is fixing something around the house. Deciding to stop putting off the task and starting it will be easier if the decision is made to see how many tries it takes to actually fix the item. Or even if the task cannot be finished, the decision to begin is important because the process of trying to fix the item will teach something new.

Go ahead and try to set some new and adventurous goals.

2. SET TIME LIMITS ON ACTIVITIES

After an individual sets new goals for life and defines the subgoals for any given set of tasks, some thought may be given to deciding how much time to spend on accomplishing each task. Then a goal would be to finish within the time limit set. An example would be setting aside an hour to run errands instead of spending all day Saturday doing it perfectly.

In chapter 6 I presented a chart that illustrates why too much effort or motivation leads to diminishing returns. The chart shows that "a middle amount of motivation results in the best performance."[5] When motivation to do a task is too low, a person may think, *I don't care . . . ; It doesn't matter. . . ;* or *I don't want to. . . .* When motivation is too high, a person may think, *I must do well; I can't goof up;* or *I will be worthless if I don't do it perfectly.* Middle levels of motivation come from these kinds of thoughts: *I would like to do this well; It would be nice if . . . ;* or *How I do this task is not a measure of my worth as a person.* Setting realistic time limits for tasks helps keep motivation at the optimal level—the middle.

When attempts to set realistic time limits on tasks produce thoughts that represent too much motivation, those thoughts can be combated and a reasonable amount of time determined to do the tasks. (I'll show how to combat those thoughts a little later on in the chapter.)

Another way to set realistic time limits is to aim too low. For instance, if it takes twenty-five minutes to drive to the office, including a stop at the post office, allow thirty minutes to complete the task. That way, even if all the lights are red, the task can still be completed within thirty minutes. The successful experience of reaching a goal will help in setting other time limits for reaching other goals.

3. ENJOY A PERSONAL TREAT

Perfectionists need to discover that joy can come from a variety of activities. For instance, one person's treat might be starting the day fifteen minutes earlier than usual by spending the time leisurely reading the paper, enjoying breakfast with the family, or walking the dog. It need not be a mad rush to start the day fifteen minutes earlier, however.

Someone else may decide to take a lunch hour and just have lunch, using the time as a respite from work.

Going somewhere nice and meeting a friend or two can add to the enjoyment. The commitment to keep lunch hours for lunch and for personal time, not for work, is a worthy one for the perfectionist with workaholic tendencies.

Sometimes it is very difficult for perfectionists to know what activities will give them pleasure. For so many years they have pushed themselves to do what they *should* do that deciding what they would *like* to do isn't easy. One way to begin is to make a list of activities that could be pleasurable. The level of performance that would have to be achieved to enjoy each activity doesn't even need to be considered in this list-making process.

The next step is to start doing some of those things. David Burns has developed a Pleasure-Perfection Balance Sheet in which he predicts how satisfying an activity will be, and then after the activity, he evaluates again how pleasurable the activity actually was. Figure 8 is an example of a sheet that a physician did.

If you would like to set up your own balance sheet, follow these simple steps. List some activities you think you might enjoy in the first column. In the second column, estimate how much pleasure you think you will get out of each one. The range is from 100 percent, or maximal pleasure and satisfaction, to 0 percent, or no pleasure or satisfaction at all.

After completing each activity, record how satisfying the activity actually proved to be. Record this with your comments in column three. Finally, in column four,

A PLEASURE-PERFECTION BALANCE SHEET[6]

Activity	Predict how satisfying the activity will be	Record how satisfying it actually was	Record how effectively you performed
Fix broken pipe in kitchen	20%	99% (I actually did it.)	20% (I took a long time and made a lot of mistakes.)
Give lecture to medical school class	70%	50% (I didn't feel particularly gratified at my performance.)	98% (As usual, I got a standing ovation.)
Play squash with Joe	75%	90% (Even though I didn't play especially well, we had a good time.)	40% (I played subpar. So what!)
Jog to store and get ice cream cone	60%	90% (It was fun!)	50% (I did not improve my time for jogging this distance.)

Fig. 8.

rate your competence in each instance, along with any comments. Like the physician, you may find that the greatest satisfaction comes from doing something new in which you do not have very much competence.

It is important for perfectionists to make these lists and create and work out these charts because they can get a more objective look at what they have been telling themselves and what has kept them from doing these things. To get started, they might actually schedule some of the things from their pleasure list as well as some activities that they have been putting off for some reason or other. They can keep working on these sheets until they are able to do the exercise automatically.

Another way to enjoy a treat is to refuse to give in to

a compulsive habit associated with perfectionism. Jane wouldn't need to go back and change her dress for the third time. She could decide to wear what she has on. George wouldn't need to drive back home to make sure the lights are off or the dog is out—he probably checked several times before he left. He chould give himself permission *not* to go back and check.

When perfectionists start to do this, they will experience a wide range of anxiety about what they are refusing to do. But they must keep refusing, and the fear will subside. They will get through and beyond it.

4. DON'T TAKE TV AND ADVERTISING TOO SERIOUSLY

A lot of what people believe about themselves is shaped by what they see on TV and what they read in ads. Few families resemble the Waltons or the Cosbys. Those families exist only on TV. I saw a part of a program recently in which the son had been watching an idealized family program on TV. (That is, in the TV program I was watching, a character was watching another TV program.) He was very upset that things in his family did not work out as they did in the TV family he was watching. The mother told him quite firmly that real-life problems don't get solved in thirty minutes. Of course, that program was on for an hour, so she could solve her family problems in sixty minutes.

I like cars, especially old ones. I enjoy going to car auctions and sitting there dreaming about how it would be to own one of those rare old beauties. In between the auctions, I look at the ads for the new cars. It's amazing how beautiful ads can make them look. The car I want is the one that looks the sleekest in the most recent ad I read.

Several years ago, I had the opportunity to buy a classic—a 1965 Mustang convertible. To my dismay, I discovered that wanting to own one was far more satisfying than actually owning one. My experience proved to be a good example of the conflict between the real and the ideal. The idea of owning one of these cars was far more exciting than the reality of owning one. But then, that's the way advertising is supposed to work.

A friend helped Jan and me with this recently. He suggested to us, as he has with all his other clients, that we make a list of everything we own. Once the list was made, he told us to go through it and ask two questions about each item: (1) Do we need it? and (2) How does it add meaning to our lives? As we went through this exercise, we were amazed at how many things we have that we don't need or that do not add any meaning to our lives. Now when I look at an old car or a new car ad, I ask myself whether I need that car or not. Then I ask how it would add meaning to my life. Those ads on TV and in the magazines have simply lost their power over me.

5. WORK ON THOUGHT PATTERNS

Our thoughts are responsible for how we feel and most of what we do. Events occur in our lives, and we usually blame what we feel or how we act on these events. But events, as they are perceived by us, are interpreted in our thoughts. This inner conversation with ourselves is what causes us to feel what we feel and do much of what we do. Our experiences are processed in our thoughts and given meaning *before* we feel a certain way or respond in a certain way.

Perfectionism, as we have already seen, has as part of its style certain thought patterns that place demands on perfectionists, who in turn place demands on others. If they are going to break free from the behavioral patterns, they need to work on the belief patterns that are associated with their perfectionism.

One way to understand this better is to create a worksheet to help identify thought patterns.

WHEN THIS HAPPENS →	I THINK THIS	→ AND DO THIS
When there are clothes on the floor after the kids leave for school . . .	*What if someone comes by and sees this mess and thinks I'm a horrible housekeeper and a terrible mother* . . . (all-or-nothing thinking).	I compulsively put everything away immediately.
When something I have on doesn't match perfectly under some light . . .	*People will think that I'm a slob who doesn't know how to dress or match color and that I must be blind* . . . (maximizing and minimizing).	I change clothes for the third time this morning.
My sister is upset that I didn't do what she expected me to do. . . .	*I can't stand it when anyone is unhappy with me. Everyone must always like me* . . . (irrational demands).	I "fake" it so she won't know I'm upset by her attitude. I tell her it is okay, even though it is not.
Someone has asked me to do something, and I don't have the time to do it.	*If I am a good person, I will try to help people. I want people to like me, so I can't say no. After all, that's selfish* (all-or-nothing thinking).	I stay up late, taking time away from myself and my family to do something I resent doing.

Fig. 9.

Notice that the sheet has three columns; the left one is labeled "When This Happens"; the middle, "I Think This"; and the right, "And Do This." Starting with the left column, record events that trigger perfectionistic behavior, and in the right column, examples of perfectionistic behavior. When both columns are filled in, the kinds of thoughts that maintain these behaviors are identified in the middle column.

Now fill in your own worksheet:

WHEN THIS HAPPENS →	I THINK THIS	→ AND DO THIS

Fig. 10.

Another helpful exercise involves making a list of all the advantages and all the disadvantages of attempts at perfection. Most perfectionists who do this exercise honestly end up with rather lopsided lists like the one here. The minuses far outweigh the pluses.

ADVANTAGES OF PERFECTIONISM	DISADVANTAGES OF PERFECTIONISM
I appear to be responsible to other people. I do a better job than others most of the time. I am a *good* employee.	I have a lot of unfinished things because I am afraid not to do a perfect job. Frustration! I get knots in my stomach when the deadline comes and I'm not finished. I can be very defensive about things I do. I'm afraid to try new things because I won't be able to do them perfectly. I put off doing things and have lots of excuses. I have the ability to do things but can never really enjoy doing them because of the tension. I worry a lot about what other people think. I don't even know, sometimes, what I think.

Fig. 11.

When perfectionists run these kinds of balance sheets, they can learn new thought patterns, or belief systems, about perfectionism that they can use to combat their perfectionistic thought patterns.

Throughout this book we have discussed the dichotomous thinking pattern, the all-or-nothing pattern, that perfectionists practice. As they work on self-talk, it is important for them to challenge these irrational patterns of thinking. One way to do this is to spend some time examining the all-or-nothing thoughts on the worksheet created like the one just described. For example, let's look at the first thought on our sample: *What if someone comes by and sees this mess and thinks I'm a horrible housekeeper and a terrible mother?* This woman could ask herself if these statements are really true. Is she really a horrible housekeeper and a terrible mother? Is her house *always* a mess? Is it a pigpen? Is it totally dirty and messy? Or is it sometimes a mess but usually in good order?

Or take the thought, *Everyone must always like me.* Is that possible? Can *everyone* in the whole world really like her at *all* times? Is it even possible for *everyone* who knows her to like her *all* the time? Is it possible that sometimes others are neutral about her? Isn't it possible for others to be angry with her and still like her—sometimes?

As perfectionists go through these mental steps, they will find it increasingly difficult to keep their world neatly divided into two categories—all good or all bad.

Another way to attack these thought patterns is to try to imagine the worst that can happen. Let's say that someone unexpectedly drops by the perfectionist's house just after the kids leave for school and finds the house a mess and her all ragged and frazzled. The uninvited guest berates her for all her inadequacies, telling her what an awful person she is. Not only that, but the outspoken individual writes an article about her in the newspaper so that everyone in town will know how awful she is. The article is picked up by the evening news on TV, and the president is watching. Now he knows how awful she is. Soon, everyone in the world knows, and the perfectionist has no place to hide. How awful! How catastrophic! How ridiculous! What are the chances that someone will stop by in such circumstances? One in a hundred? What are the chances that any of the rest of that scenario would happen? None!

A technique used by some who work on their perfectionism in a group is to suggest that persons take an upcoming activity or time period in which they will attempt to conduct themselves perfectly. They are to decide that *everything* that occurs in that space of time will be perfect. Of course, the moment someone attempts to do something perfectly, the attempt will fail. That's the way a paradox works. When people do this in a group, the reports can be quite amusing because the technique shows how ridiculous attempts at perfection really are.

As a follow-up to the attempt to do everything perfectly within a block of time, the group then suggests that persons deliberately decide to take a block of time, or an upcoming activity, and give themselves permission to make mistakes. It is important that they do not deliberately make mistakes, simply give themselves permission to make them. Usually, when the two occasions are compared and discussed within the group, the performance is of a better quality and more satisfying when people have given themselves permission to make mistakes.

A helpful exercise for perfectionists is to work on the worksheet dealing with thought patterns from a non-perfectionistic point of view. Notice the changes in this approach:

WHEN THIS HAPPENS →	I THINK THIS →	AND DO THIS
When there are clothes on the floor after the kids leave for school . . .	*What a mess! That's kids. It would be nice if they'd learn to pick up their things. It sure doesn't mean the whole house is dirty.*	I'm going to take a moment for myself and relax with a cup of coffee.
When something I have on doesn't match perfectly under some light . . .	*Most people don't see what I see in colors. I can explain if someone says something, or if I feel uncomfortable.*	If I have time I will change, or take the time later to look for something that matches the outfit.
My sister is upset that I didn't do what she expected me to do. . . .	*I blew it, but life continues. I am not perfect.*	I will apologize and work out some compromise so both of us are okay about it.
Someone has asked me to do something, and I don't have the time to do it . . .	*I know I am a good person whether I say yes or no. This person asking me will probably understand.*	I say no and tell the person to ask me again to help in the future.

Fig. 12.

When they think in nonperfectionistic patterns, they will find that they have a lot more energy. They will have started the process of breaking free from the prison of perfection.

6. SHARE THE PROCESS AND
THE PROGRESS

It's important for perfectionists to share the process of what they are doing with someone they trust or even with a group of people who have agreed to meet together to work on their perfectionism. A good way for an individual to begin is to discuss feelings of nervousness about working on perfectionism with another perfectionistic friend. The pair might agree to read this book and meet for lunch once a week to talk about reactions to the reading.

This step is different from the suggestion in the last chapter about what to do with the things written in a journal. Here, I am suggesting that the perfectionist get together with another person or a group of people who will actively work on the task of breaking old behavior patterns.

If a group of people is going to be involved, here are some suggestions for things to do in the meetings. The same things will work just as well with two people, but a group of eight or ten will add some fun and insight to the process.

First, spend some time to *clarify the goals* of the group. Include in these goals each individual's desire to become more comfortable with personal imperfection. Then work on the goals each person has reset, based on the material in the first section of this chapter. In the discussions about individual goals, help one another see any hidden pockets of residual perfectionism, and try to reword goals so that they are free of perfectionism. As everyone shares newly restated goals, a feeling of mutual accountability is promoted. There is strength in numbers, as long as the group isn't much larger than eight or ten.

Second, use the group to help participants *become aware of patterns* in behavior that set them up for perfectionism. Share perfectionism worksheets or lists of advantages and disadvantages of perfectionism. As these are discussed, ask expansive questions: "In what other situations do you think the same way?" or "Are there other times when you find yourself responding like that?" It is amazing how a group of people working on the same problem can help one another find the blind spots that can often sabotage the efforts of the individual.

Third, look for what are known as *secondary gains.* These are like the side benefits we receive from acting certain ways. In any part of life, "any longstanding cognitive pattern is not easily dismissed, particularly when it has been mistakenly viewed as the reason for one's success."[7] That is to say that all behavior is purposive. There is a reason for why we do things. Being willing to look at the "whys" of their thought and behavior patterns will help people evaluate just how free they are to changing those patterns and will also help them face how strong their desire is to make the changes. The accountability of the group needs to be loving and understanding so that each member is willing to continue to participate.

Fourth, the group will help members *confront thought patterns.* Much of it is going on unconsciously. That is, people are not even aware of what they are saying to themselves part of the time. It is interesting to me in therapy that after I have talked with someone about this, all I need to do is ask "What?" and the individual pauses. Usually, the person catches it quickly, laughs about it, and then changes the way of saying things. A key word to watch for with perfectionists is *should.* We've talked about the effects of this word and how it can control behavior. Other words like *should* include *ought, must, never, always,* and their negative counterparts. Help one another hear what is really being said, and confront perfectionistic self-talk.

Fifth, create a balanced perspective in each participant's world. A between-sessions assignment can be to find posters, ads, or mottos that reflect the perfectionistic attitudes of our culture and then rewrite them in a way that reflects balance. One person saw a poster that said, "Put your time to maximum use." She decided to reword it to say, "Make sure you save time to play."

Spend time discussing how some regular activities can be done in nonperfectionistic ways. If someone has been a perfectionist about an exercise program, talk about how he can have more of a balance in this part of his life. Perhaps he can exercise with a friend or become more flexible about when he exercises.

Another aspect of balance is to undertake new activities. As we have discussed, perfectionists avoid doing many things because they can't do them perfectly. The group can help members gain the courage to take the risk and do something different. Eventually, each participant would be able to talk about doing something new.

As people break perfectionistic behavior patterns, they will begin to feel much better about themselves, and they will begin an adventure of discovering new and enjoyable things. It's a lot more fun being human than trying to be perfect. Everything we have talked about in this chapter is a process. No one can ever be a perfect nonperfectionist—there is no such thing. In this process of becoming less perfectionistic, individuals can become more fully human and enjoy it because it's a lifetime endeavor.

Perfectly Human

> *One's natural instinct is to strive for*
> *godlikeness, because one does not have*
> *the "courage to be imperfect."*
> —*Paul Rom*

*I*t seems clear by now that "perfectionism inhibits human growth and saps our capacity for delighting in life. And the great demand of religion is, of course, 'Be ye perfect!'"[1] Many of us believe that God demands that we be perfect, just as he is perfect. One man asks me almost weekly, "But what will God think?" He is struggling with the conflict between who he really is and who he is trying to be to gain God's approval. His question is real, arising from the depths of his inner fears. For this man, God not only demands perfection, but is keeping close tabs on how he is doing; some day God will check the balance sheet to see if he measured up.

It is no wonder that people who have an image of God as a "spiritual terrorist" shy away from him. Canon Holmes of India called attention to the inferential character of the average person's concept of God:

To most people God is an inference, not a reality. He is a deduction from evidence which they consider adequate; but He remains personally unknown to the individual. . . . They have never bothered to think the matter out for themselves, but have heard about Him from others, and have put belief in Him into the back of their minds along with the various odds and ends that make up their total creed. To many others God is but an ideal, another name for goodness, or beauty, or truth; or He is law, or life, or the creative impulse back of the phenomena of existence. These notions about God . . . have one thing in common: they do not know God in personal experience.[2]

I've found this to be true even with people who are very serious about their faith. Their concepts of God are based on what other people have told them, not on their own research. They have listened to the ideas of preachers and teachers or have had their picture of God shaped by their parents. So often, the perfectionist lives with a God who acts very much like a critical, demanding parent. One perfectionist remarked:

Since God demands perfection, I can see every day where I fall short of His standards. My family and friends know me well enough to tolerate my inconsistencies and imperfections, but not God.

This image of God can be experienced, even though intellectually the person knows God's acceptance. An example is the person who said:

My perfectionism affects my relationship with God. I don't know what He wants, what He expects. I don't know how productive I am in His eyes. I don't see my value before God, yet I know His Word says that I have ultimate value to Him. I don't feel it, can't see it, don't know if I want to.

THE PROCESS OF REDEFINING GOD

For this person, as well as for most perfectionists, the experience of change in the area of perfectionism will require a redefinition of God. This does not mean that they should come up with some new image of God. What it does mean is that they must redefine their past image of God in terms of how he presents himself in the Bible. Over against the distorted images of a "terrorist God"

stands the clear scriptural doctrine that God can be known in personal experience. A loving Personality dominates the Bible, walking among the trees of the garden and breathing fragrance over every scene. Always a living Person is present, speaking, pleading, loving, working and manifesting Himself whenever and wherever His people have the receptivity necessary to receive the manifestation.[3]

It's hard for perfectionists to see God in this way. They define God in terms of the all-or-nothing dichotomy: He is all-good (which God is), and they are all-bad. They believe that they must somehow become perfect to relate to God. One perfectionist said, "If I don't do everything I think is right, I feel guilty and find it hard to relate to God." She sees God as the critical, punishing parent, attaching to him attitudes she experienced with her own parents. When I asked her if she was that kind of parent to her son, she quickly protested with a firm, "No!" Even though she was trying to be the perfect, loving parent, she couldn't see God in this loving parental role.

Jesus asked:

What man is there among you who, if his son asks for bread, will give him a stone? Or if he asks for a fish, will he give him a serpent? If you then, being evil, know how to give good gifts to your children, how much more will your Father who is in heaven give good things to those who ask Him! (Matt. 7:9–11).

The tendency of perfectionists is to read those verses and say, "Yes, but. . . ." And after the "but" comes the list of things that they must do to "deserve" whatever God wants to give them.

Joseph R. Cooke, professor of anthropology at the University of Washington, paid a great price for his perfectionistic attitudes about God. In his book, *Free for the Taking*, he relates how, as a missionary in Thailand, he created an impossible God. The God he served was different from the God he taught others about; his God made impossible demands of him. He writes:

> **His opinion of me was so low, there was no way for me to live except under His frown. . . . All day long He nagged me. "Why don't you pray more? Why don't you witness more? When will you ever learn self-discipline? How can you allow yourself to indulge in such wicked thoughts? Do this. Don't do that. Yield, confess, work harder." . . . Most of all, I had a God who down underneath considered me to be less than dirt. . . . When I came down to it, there was scarcely a word, or a feeling, or a thought, or a decision of mine that God really liked.[4]**

His frustration became more and more intense until, finally, he had to leave Thailand because he had a complete emotional breakdown.

His experience is not unique. I am working with several people right now who are perfectionistic in their attitudes about God and about life. One of their main concerns is whether or not they are still sane. They are running as fast as they can on the treadmill of their perfectionism, and God is the One who keeps turning up the speed. He's the One demanding that they run faster. They desperately need to redefine God.

For Cooke and for most perfectionists, God sits in his heaven, keeping track of who does what. When they think of God seeing them, they become nervous, uncomfortable, wishing for a place to hide. They have no personal knowledge of the kind of God described by Tozer, who said:

> **When we lift our inward eyes to gaze upon God we are sure to meet friendly eyes gazing back at us, for it is written that the eyes of the Lord run to and fro throughout all the earth. The sweet language of experience is "Thou, God, seest me." When the eyes of the soul looking out meet the eyes of God looking in, heaven has begun right here on this earth.[5]**

Instead, for perfectionists, God's eyes are filled with judgment.

I often ask people I counsel to read chapters 5 through 8 of Romans at one sitting, once a day for thirty days. It seems to be a common experience that if individuals do something once a day for thirty days, it becomes a part of them. If perfectionists can get all four chapters to become a part of them, they will have taken giant steps in the process of redefining God.

In the fifth chapter of Romans, Paul used three words to describe us: *ungodly, sinners, enemies.* Although we were like this, Paul said that "Christ died for us" (v. 8). And because it is so profound, he added, "We also rejoice in God through our Lord Jesus Christ, through whom we have now received the reconciliation" (v. 11). We were the enemies of God, but He made it possible for us to be reconciled to Him. Now that we are his friends, how much more will he freely give to us! That's God's nature—he doesn't demand, he freely gives.

The whole truth that Paul wanted us to experience is that we have been set free from the legalism of the law to a spirit of love. Our relationship with God is not based on perfection. It is based on confession: "If we confess our sins, He is faithful and just to forgive us our sins and to cleanse us from all unrighteousness" (1 John 1:9).

David Seamands claims that perfectionism is a counterfeit for wholeness, "holiness, sanctification, or the Spirit-filled life. Instead of making us holy persons and integrated personalities—that is, whole persons in Christ—perfectionism leaves us spiritual Pharisees and emotional neurotics."[6] Perfectionism distorts God, denying any connection with the loving, forgiving Father in the Bible.

THE PROCESS OF NURTURING
THE REAL SELF

If perfectionists are to allow the real self to develop and grow, they need somewhere in life to experience unconditional love. Carl Rogers said that in order to be a person, one needs an experience of unconditional positive regard. But life isn't that way. Life is full of conditions. That's where God as the unconditional lover comes so powerfully into the picture. If perfectionists create an image of a God who demands that they meet impossible standards and withholds love when they fall short, they have effectively eliminated the real God.

This is the heart of the parable of the prodigal son (see Luke 15:11–32). The younger son wants to stand on his own two feet. He wants to break free from the demands of his father and make it on his own. So he goes in the face of tradition, takes his inheritance, and leaves. He doesn't do well; eventually, he ends up feeding pigs and eating their leftovers. He determines to head home and become a slave in his father's home. He has lost himself, along with all his dreams of grandeur. He has come to the end of his ideal self and is willing to face his real self, even if that means being a slave.

What he doesn't expect is his father's reaction to his return. The father in the parable is a picture of God the Father. So like God, the father's eyes run to and fro across the landscape, longing for his son's eyes to meet his. The father's eyes are filled with love, not judgment; with acceptance, not conditions. And when that glorious day arrives and the son returns, the father, in his unconditional love, welcomes the young man home as a beloved son, not as a slave.

Helmut Thielicke refers to an idea about this parable presented by André Gide. He has the returned

prodigal sending his brother out into the far country so that he, too, can "grow up" and mature. What Gide is really saying is that it was good for the lost son to be lost for a while.

It was good for him to sin. After all, a person has to go through this kind of thing. And one must have the courage to renounce God in order that one may be accepted by him afterward. The son has simply experienced to the full the fruitful polarity of life.[7]

One does not have to sin boldly to experience this polarity—this balance—in life. But one may renounce the god of one's own making to experience the full and unconditional acceptance of the God of reality. This experience of acceptance for the prodigal was a fresh affirmation of the acceptance that had always been there for him. When it became his, he was a new man! His real self came alive.

For the perfectionist, this is difficult to accept. A woman told me of a disturbing dream she had. She was in the lobby of a hotel. There were an old man and a woman working behind the desk. She was upset because she kept hearing a mother beating her child and the child screaming for help. Finally, she went up to the woman at the desk and asked if she could help the child. The woman replied, "No, this is something that he will take care of." And with that, the old man went to solve the problem. The dream ended as she watched the woman carrying the little girl, who was sobbing quietly, out of the hotel.

I suggested that she write about the dream in her journal and attempt to carry on an imaginary conversation with each person in the dream to find out more about its meaning. She asked the mother her name and was told, "I'm your perfectionism." The mother also told her that the child's name was "the new you," and "I'm trying to beat her into shape." She asked the name of the woman behind the desk and was told, "I'm the traffic director." She also was told that the old man was sent to help because she (the person dreaming) was not able to help.

Then she asked the old man his name and was told, "My name is 'Wise-Doer.'" When she asked what that meant, he said, "I don't think. I just do."

I find it interesting that we had not been discussing this woman's perfectionism. We were looking at some of the roots of her behavior, and during the period of time when we were having those discussions, she had the dream about her perfectionism. She was a mature Christian who worked very hard at doing everything just right. In that process, she had developed the pattern of always analyzing her actions, often delaying doing something so that she could better analyze it. I commented on the old man's name of "Wise-Doer" and suggested that she might try just doing things without analyzing them, for the message of the dream seemed to include the idea that she already was a very wise person. Her problem was that she often didn't trust God's wisdom at work within her. Since that dream, she has acted on things without analyzing them so much, and she is feeling a new sense of freedom from her perfectionism.

Another woman, when asked to look at a rose and

simply enjoy its beauty, turned away with tears, asking, "What's the point of doing that? It's a waste of time." She's the opposite of the woman with the dream. Instead of waiting and analyzing before doing, this woman just keeps busy doing. But both of them avoid looking at their real selves, afraid to trust the inner wisdom there—the loving wisdom of God placed within them by God's Holy Spirit. Both women are unsure of that inner wisdom—afraid that it might not be God's voice within. They are not quite convinced that they are worthy of God's unconditional love.

King David, in the Old Testament, is an encouragement to those who can't quite accept the fact that God's love is unconditional. He was perfectly human. He sinned badly, and the pages of the Bible make no attempt to conceal his flaws. He lusted after a woman, committed adultery with her, murdered her husband, and struggled deeply with his role as a father. In the midst of his sin, he did not set himself up to try to win God's approval. Instead, he confessed his failure and focused on God's unconditional love of him. Psalm 51 presents some of his thoughts:

> **Have mercy upon me, O God,**
> **According to Your lovingkindness;**
> **According to the multitude of Your tender**
> **   mercies,**
> **Blot out my transgressions.**
> **Wash me thoroughly from my iniquity,**
> **And cleanse me from my sin. . . .**
> **Behold, You desire truth in the inward parts,**

And in the hidden part You will make me to
know wisdom. . . .
Create in me a clean heart, O God,
And renew a steadfast spirit within me.
Do not cast me away from Your presence,
And do not take Your Holy Spirit from me.
Restore to me the joy of Your salvation,
And uphold me by Your generous Spirit
(vv. 1-2, 6, 10-12).

God, in his unconditional love of David, graciously an-
swered his prayer. The apostle Paul referred to David
and pointed out that God said, "I have found David the
son of Jesse, a man after My own heart, who will do all
My will" (Acts 13:22). God is a loving, forgiving God. It
is his nature to love without condition.

If perfectionists are afraid of sinning too boldly,
Romans 6 will provide a balance point because Paul
talked about that fear. In chapter 7, he talked about the
opposite fear—the fear of not doing it perfectly.

The person who is setting the real self free and is
breaking the bondage of perfectionism will redefine
God so that His true nature can be understood and experienced. "God is a Person, and in the deep of His
mighty nature He thinks, wills, enjoys, feels, loves, desires and suffers as any other person may."[8] Discover
that God—the real God—and nurture the real self under the care of his unconditional love.

THE PROCESS OF CHANGING
ONE'S LIFE

One perfectionist wrote about the effect of this discovery: "I'm glad now that God is perfect! Because I also know that He is perfect in His forgiveness, His grace, and His mercy."

David Seamands says:

> **There is only one ultimate cure for perfectionism: it is profound and yet as simple as the word _grace_. In the New Testament, this word has a special meaning: "freely given, undeserved, unmerited, unearnable, and unrepayable favor." It means that God's loving acceptance of us has nothing to do with our worthiness, nothing to do with what we deserve.[9]**

The first words of Romans 8 are words of release: "There is therefore now no condemnation to those who are in Christ Jesus" (v. 1). Nothing can condemn us! Wow! But Paul was just getting started. He added, "What then shall we say to these things? If God is for us, who can be against us?" (v. 31). If he were writing for perfectionists, he might have worded it like this: "If God is for us, how dare _we_ be against us!" He went on:

> **Who shall bring a charge against God's elect? It is God who justifies. Who is he who condemns? . . . Who shall separate us from the**

love of Christ? . . . I am persuaded that neither
death nor life, nor angels nor principalities nor
powers, nor things present nor things to come,
nor height nor depth, nor any other created
thing, shall be able to separate us from the
love of God (vv. 33–35, 38–39).

Nothing in *all* of creation can separate us from God's
loving, unconditional acceptance of us! That covers
everything. To perfectionists, this means living in a
both-and world instead of an either-or world. It means
that they can be both good and bad and still be lovingly
accepted by God. They can fail and succeed, let people
down, let God down, and still be lovingly accepted. One
perfectionist said:

I started to feel free of perfectionism with the
realization that my faith explains *why* I can
appreciate perfection (I'm created in the
image of a perfect God), and why I fall short of
achieving that perfection (sin), and that God
eternally vests me with worth. It's His gift to
me, just as wealth and status are gifts, not
something earned.

He sees God's grace accurately. It is God's gift that cannot in any way possibly be earned.

The process of breaking free from perfectionism is
similar to the recovery process for the chemically de-
pendent, which requires people to live one day at a
time. That means that each day is the only part of the

process they can see and affect, so they are satisfied with growth that comes in small steps. Brian L. writes of his recovery as a daily recognition that his worth was not measured by the perfection of his behavior and actions. By growing spiritually, he realized that

> **even when our actions seem perfect we would be wise to remember that we remain imperfect human beings. . . . Perfection is a subjective, abstract ideal few people agree on. . . . If we impatiently pursue abstractions such as perfection and happiness in our lives, we probably will be too distracted to enjoy the smaller pleasures and satisfactions that come our way. If we are living for today, we will take the time to find and appreciate experiences that give our lives more joy and meaning than any perfect achievements could give us.**[10]

Changing the lifestyle of perfectionists is a lifetime challenge that progresses one day at a time. The process includes:

- *One day at a time,* spiritually rediscovering God as he really is, not as he is imagined to be.

- *One day at a time,* going through the pain of discovering the real self by experiencing and enjoying the unconditional love and acceptance made available by a loving God.

- *One day at a time,* experiencing forgiveness while living in the reality of that loving and gracious forgiveness freely offered by God.

- *One day at a time,* learning to listen to the inner wisdom from God, trusting it for release to be loving and forgiving persons.

Perfectionists have been described as "people with lives rich in achievement but poor in joy."[11] It doesn't have to be that way. The ultimate challenge for perfectionists is to see that happiness and acceptance are a way of life, not merely a goal. True joy is a by-product of experiencing acceptance and forgiveness and of being accepting and forgiving persons as well. Enjoy the challenge!

Perfectionist Prayer

Dear God, help me to accept my human limitations and know that you accept me just as I am. Give me the courage to forgive and be forgiven, and to trust that inner wisdom placed within me by your Holy Spirit. Help me to celebrate life as you have given it to me. Amen.

NOTES

Chapter One

1. Karen Horney, *Neurosis and Human Growth* (New York: Norton, 1950), pp. 64ff.
2. See David Burns, "The Perfectionist's Script for Self-Defeat," *Psychology Today* (November 1980): 44.
3. David Burns, *Feeling Good* (New York: Morrow, 1980), p. 390.
4. Brian L., *Perfectionism* (Center City, Minn.: Hazelden, 1985), p. 7.

Chapter Two

1. Emanuel M. Berger, "Irrational Self-Censure: The Problem and Its Correction," *Personnel and Guidance Journal* 53 (November 1974): 194.

2. John C. Barrow and Carol A. Moore, "Group Interventions with Perfectionistic Thinking," *Personnel and Guidance Journal* (June 1983): 613.
3. Aaron T. Beck, A. John Rush, Brian F. Shaw, and Gary Emery, *Cognitive Therapy of Depression* (New York: Guilford Press, 1979), p. 14.
4. Berger, "Irrational Self-Censure," p. 194.
5. John R. Snortum, "Ben Franklin's Pursuit of Perfection," *Psychology Today* (April 1976): 82.
6. Ibid., p. 83.
7. Paul Rom, "The Misery of Perfectionism," *Individual Psychologist* 8 (May 1971): 18.
8. David A. Seamands, *Healing for Damaged Emotions* (Wheaton, Ill.: Victor Books, 1981), p. 80.
9. Burns, "Perfectionist's Script," p. 37.
10. Abby A. Belson, "The Perfection Principle: Are You Too Good for Your Own Good?" *Mademoiselle* (September 1984): 310.
11. Charles M. Kelly, "Reasonable Performance Appraisals," *Training and Development Journal* 30 (January 1984): 79.
12. E. Laird Landon, Jr., "Self Concept, Ideal Self Concept, and Consumer Purchase Intentions," *Journal of Consumer Research* 1 (September 1974): 44–51.
13. Suzanne McNear, "The Curse of Perfectionism," *Cosmopolitan* (October 1981): 296.
14. Barrow and Moore, "Group Interventions," p. 612.

Chapter Three

1. Berger, "Irrational Self-Censure," p. 196.
2. Ibid.

3. Paul Watzlawick, "The Pathologies of Perfectionism," *Etc.* 34 (March 1977): 13.
4. Ibid.
5. Ibid.
6. Ibid.
7. Thomas J. Peters and Robert H. Waterman, *In Search of Excellence* (New York: Harper & Row, 1982), pp. 20, 21.
8. Ibid.
9. Horney, *Neurosis*, p. 176.
10. Virginia Hall and Joyce Wessel, "Perfectionism is not always the perfect answer," *The Atlanta Journal*, December 2, 1984, p. 63.
11. Edward J. Bride, "The Tragedy of Driven People," *Software News* (September 1985): 6.
12. Kerry McPhedran, "Are You Trying Too Hard to Be Perfect?" *New Woman* (July 1985): 54.
13. Joseph R. Cooke, *Free for the Taking* (Old Tappan, N.J.: Revell, 1975), p. 46.
14. McNear, "Curse of Perfectionism," p. 295.
15. Grant Howard, *Balancing Life's Demands: A New Perspective on Priorities* (Portland: Multnomah Press, 1983), p. 19.

Chapter Four

1. Horney, *Neurosis*, p. 18.
2. Quoted in Harold I. Kaplan, Alfred M. Freedman, and Benjamin J. Sadock, eds., *Comprehensive Textbook of Psychiatry*, vol. 1 (Baltimore: Williams & Wilkins, 1980), p. 743.
3. Althea J. Horner, *Object Relations and the Develop-*

ing Ego in Therapy (New York: Jason Aronson, 1984), p. 102.

4. Arnold Rothstein, "An Exploration of the Diagnostic Term 'Narcissistic Personality Disorder,'" *Journal of the American Psychoanalytic Association* 27, no. 4 (1979): 905.
5. Horney, *Neurosis*, p. 25.
6. Ibid., pp. 64, 65.
7. Ibid., p. 29.
8. Gloria Rakita Leon, Philip C. Kendall, and Judy Garber, "Depression in Children: Parent, Teacher, and Child Perspectives," *Journal of Abnormal Child Psychology* 8, no. 2 (1980): 221.

Chapter Five

1. Mike Mason, *The Mystery of Marriage* (Portland: Multnomah Press, 1985), p. 41.
2. Ibid.
3. Horney, *Neurosis*, p. 154.
4. Ibid., p. 39.
5. Cooke, *Free for the Taking*, p. 46.
6. David A. Seamands, "Perfectionism: Fraught with Fruits of Self-Destruction," *Christianity Today* (April 10, 1981): 24.
7. Ibid., p. 25.

Chapter Six

1. McNear, "Curse of Perfectionism," p. 296.
2. Guy R. Banta and David P. Kosnosky, "Case Report

of an Obsessive-Compulsive Personality: A Precursor to Accident Proneness," *Aviation, Space, and Environmental Medicine* (June 1978): 827, 828.
3. Betty Uniberti, "Obsessive-Compulsives Tied to Parents," *Los Angeles Times*, February 8, 1983.
4. Nathan E. Rickles, "The Angry Woman Syndrome," *Archives of General Psychiatry* 24 (January 1971): 91.
5. Burns, "Perfectionist's Script," p. 41.
6. William D. Criddle, "Don't Try Too Hard!" *Rational Living* 10, no. 2 (1975): 19.
7. Patricia Reid Eldridge, "Karen Horney and Clarissa: The Tragedy of Neurotic Pride," *The American Journal of Psychoanalysis* 42, no. 1 (1982): 55.
8. McNear, "Curse of Perfectionism," p. 319.
9. Burns, "Perfectionist's Script," p. 34.

Chapter Seven

1. Quoted in Mary Miles, "Type A Personality: Bad Business?" *Computer Decisions* (April 1984): 188.
2. Quoted in Susan Wels, "Children Under Stress," *The Stanford Magazine* (Summer 1985): 30.
3. McPhedran, "Are You Trying Too Hard?" p. 55.
4. John S. Tamerin and Charles P. Neuman, "The Alcoholic Stereotype: Clinical Reappraisal and Implications for Treatment," *The American Journal of Psychoanalysis* 34, no. 4 (1974): 317.
5. Ibid., p. 318.
6. John S. Tamerin and Charles P. Neuman, "Psychological Aspects of Treating Alcoholism," *Alcohol Health and Research World* (Spring 1974): 17.
7. Brian L., *Perfectionism*, p. 2.

8. Ibid., p. 5.
9. John D. McCann, "The Destructive Element of Perfectionism as Evidenced in Alcoholism," *Pastoral Psychology* 22, no. 2 (1971): 26.
10. Ada Holub and Maria Kazubska, "Mental Disorders in Patients with Ulcerative Colitis," *Polish Medical Journal* 5, no. 1 (1971): 1497–1501.
11. David P. Smith et al., "A Psychiatric Study of Atypical Facial Pain," *Canadian Medical Association Journal* 100, no. 6 (1969): 286–90.
12. Michael C. Quadland, "Private Self-consciousness, Attribution of Responsibility, and Perfectionistic Thinking in Secondary Erectile Dysfunction," *Journal of Sex and Marital Therapy* 6, no. 1 (1980): 47–55.
13. Warren L. McNab, "Anorexia and the Adolescent," *Journal of School Health* 53, no. 7 (1983): 427–30.
14. David M. Garner and Paul E. Garfinkel, eds., *Handbook of Psychotherapy for Anorexia Nervosa and Bulimia* (New York: Guilford Press, 1985), p. 128.

Chapter Eight

1. Horney, *Neurosis*, p. 305.
2. Ibid., pp. 177ff.
3. Ibid., p. 353.
4. Ibid., p. 183.
5. *Twelve Steps and Twelve Traditions* (New York: Alcoholics Anonymous World Services, 1952), p. 21.
6. Ibid., p. 40.
7. Horney, *Neurosis*, p. 82.
8. Carl Jung, *Answer to Job* (Princeton, N.J.: Princeton University Press, 1954), p. 33.

9. Ibid.
10. Ibid., p. 37.

Chapter Nine

1. Burns, "Perfectionist's Script," p. 44.
2. For a more detailed discussion of these principles, see my book *Self-Talk: Key to Personal Growth* (Old Tappan, N.J.: Revell, 1982).
3. Burns, "Perfectionist's Script," p. 38.
4. Horney, *Neurosis*, p. 84.
5. Criddle, "Don't Try Too Hard!" p. 19.
6. Burns, "Perfectionist's Script," p. 50.
7. Barrow and Moore, "Group Interventions," p. 614.

Chapter Ten

1. Alan W. Jones, *Soulmaking* (San Francisco: Harper & Row, 1985), p. 35.
2. A. W. Tozer, *The Pursuit of God* (Harrisburg, Pa.: Christian Publications, 1948), p. 49.
3. Ibid., p. 50.
4. Cooke, *Free for the Taking*, p. 42.
5. Tozer, *Pursuit of God*, p. 92.
6. Seamands, *Healing for Damaged Emotions*, p. 78.
7. Helmut Thielicke, *The Waiting Father* (San Francisco: Harper & Row, 1959), p. 27.
8. Tozer, *Pursuit of God*, p. 13.
9. Seamands, "Perfectionism," p. 26.
10. Brian L., *Perfectionism*, pp. 12–13.
11. Ibid.